Smart Selling

How You Can Turn Ordinary Selling Into Extraordinary Income

Twenty lessons that have helped thousands to earn millions

Stan Rosenzweig

© 2000 Stan Rosenzweig

PRINTED IN THE UNITED STATES OF AMERICA

ISBN 1-58652-000-8

Smart Selling: LCCN: 99-75933

    Publisher's Cataloging-in-Publication
    (Provided by Quality Books, Inc.)

    Rosenzweig, Stan.
    Smart selling : how you can turn ordinary
      sellinginto extraordinary income / Stan
      Rosenzweig. – 1st ed.
    p. cm.
    ISBN 1-58652-000-8

      1. Selling.   I. Title

      HF5438.25.R67 2000   658.8´5
      QBI99-1552

Books by Stan Rosenzweig

Smart Selling How You Can Turn Ordinary Selling Into Extraordinary Income. Twenty lessons that have helped thousands to earn millions.

Smart Marketing What Big Companies Practice And You Must Learn About Positioning, Branding And Other Marketing Concepts.

Smart Telemarketing How You Can Turn Ordinary Telemarketing Into Extraordinary Income.

Smart Sales Management How You Can Use The Powerful Lessons Of Others To Help You To Build And Lead A Winning Sales And Management Team.

Smart Thinking How To Use Your Own Life Experiences To Reach Greater Success. Chicken soup may be good, but front line sales experience is better.

Sailing For Non-Sailors What Every Guest Should Know Before Stepping Aboard.

Hotel Telecommunications Opportunities Through Deregulation.

Table of Contents

– Keeping the Message Simple
The KISS formula has served us well. Here's how it can do the
same for you. Examples of complex companies who have succeeded with simple messages and how to apply the concept at
home.

– How to Lose a Sale in One Easy Lesson
After winning the toughest sales, don't let the easy ones get away.
Case studies of sales that we should have, would have, could have...
but didn't.

– Shut Up and Listen
Your presentation can never compete with your prospect's internal
one. Here's the specific knowledge you need to butt in on that
silent conversation your prospect is having with himself.

– Mining Gold in Your Own Sandbox
How would you like a fresh new list of prospects you hadn't
thought of before? Two tests that will surprise you and three ways
to build new business from existing relationships.

– The Fine Art of Using References
Are you as good as you say? Who else says so? How to get references and use them to increase sales.

– The Art of the Deal
How often have you heard, "It's only a good deal if both parties are
satisfied"? Mutual satisfaction is raised to a fine art. Here's how to
bring color to your own negotiating palette.

– Direct Mail That Really Works
Did your last sales letter get lost? Or was it simply tossed? Short,
simple and easy to apply secrets to getting your next mailing read.

– Doing Business with Clients Who Hate You
Let's face it. Not everyone loves you. Can you still get them to
give you money? Three steps to getting even your most dissatisfied
customers to increase their orders.

How to get the most from this training course

· · · · ·

*T*his self paced training includes plenty of good advice to make you more successful at sales. It will help you to be more productive selling your products and services. It will help you to make more money and will help you enjoy your success.

How do I know? For one thing, I have been training sales people and sales teams for more than 25 years. I started out as an AT&T telemarketing trainer back before MCI decided to break up the phone monopoly and when every long distance phone call resulted in AT&T revenue. Our simple goal: get business to phone more often.

As AT&T PhonePower™ trainers, we would go out to visit manufacturers, truck sales companies, anyone who sold stuff, and we would teach them how to do it better over the phone...and it worked. Our customers sold more using our training assistance, so they were willing to make more phone calls. Eventually, our customers were able to create so many leads that they needed to learn how to complete the sales cycle and close more deals. So we accepted that challenge to train them in all steps of the sale.

Since then, I have helped tens of thousands of business people through seminars, books and magazine columns, including 120 sales and marketing training columns for a very popular sales publication, Reseller Management Magazine. Readers have sent me an amazing number of letters of thanks, over the years, so I know that the material I have prepared for you, here, will work.

In customizing the information in this course on selling so that it helps you to sell more, I have relied on more than years of sales training experience. I interviewed hundreds of sales people, some successful and some not so, in order to determine what sales problems you are facing in the field. I interviewed numerous people who need to sell but have no training, people who are wonderful on the technical side, but who have important questions regarding how best to increase sales.

You told me you would love to learn:

1. How to uncover greater numbers of fresh sales leads.
2. How to overcome fears prospects have regarding reliability and trust.
3. How to organize your sales calls to greatest effect.
4. How to stand up to competition from large, traditional vendors.

The 80/20 rule is wonderful when applied to sales training. It says that you derive 80% of benefit in the first 20% of the time and the remaining 20% of benefit in the remaining 80% of the time. I don't know if that is 100% true, but this sales training resource will answer your most urgent sales questions and will provide you with tools to make more sales.

80/20 notwithstanding, if you have had no prior selling experience, or if your current sales results are limited, you should consider this as a great beginning to build on, a valuable resource, but not the only resource. Read additional books and magazines on sales and marketing. Attend selling seminars. Join groups and associations comprised of sales professionals who freely exchange ideas leading to greater success.

Recognize that selling is a profession that gives forth its greatest rewards to those who continue to expand their professional understanding with time set aside, each month, to invest in its study. For those of us who do, it's a wonderful way to succeed. So, let's turn directly to Lesson One and start creating more fresh sales leads.

Why Prospects Don't Buy

. . . . .

There are five true, basic, reasons why prospects don't buy. The sooner you learn these five important reasons, the sooner you can get to the sale.

*T*here are five marketing reasons why more prospects don't buy from you. These are not sales objections, mind you. Objections are more numerous. Your prospects can come up with almost as many objections at any one sitting as President Clinton can eat cheeseburgers… That many. Objections are not the real reasons they don't buy, just reasons why your salespeople need to clarify matters.

But as for true, basic, marketing reasons for many prospects not plunking down hard-earned cash on the barrelhead and scooping up your solution, there are five. If you knew why they all don't buy, do you think you could modify your marketing strategy in order to improve your sales closing ratio? Let's see.

The first reason *you don't get a higher percentage of orders is that you haven't researched your prospects sufficiently to arrive at user-acceptable price points.*

It isn't enough to be cheaper than the competition, nor is it enough to be able to show cost-justification and relative value; you must be able to meet real and emotional pricing constraints in order to get the buyer to sign the contract. In other words, they have to know that they can afford it even if the worst-case scenario occurs.

The prospect's financial comfortability factor sometimes has less to do with your markup and profit than it has to do with the prospect's internal budgeting demands. The question may not be "Should I buy from vendor A or vendor B" but "Should I buy a new software-driven inventory control system or a new delivery truck?" Like it or not, if that's the question, the Ford dealer wins.

Pricing is not a science, but it is a marketing discipline. I have found that it is critical to determine early in the selling effort just what the prospect's financial limitations are. Then, when it is time for the proposal, you can tailor a cash purchase, lease purchase, or other funding method to the path of least resistance...but only if you understand the buyer's financial limitations and have a strategy to deal with them.

The second reason *that all of your prospects don't buy from you is because, believe it or not, all of them really don't need what you sell.*

No matter how much you pride yourself at being able to sell "ice to the Eskimos" in today's business world, if your product or service doesn't fill a void, it's a real tough, time-wasting sell.

Prospects tell your salespeople this, but, in the greater wisdom of some sales training course you took years ago, you folks believe that the prospects are lying to you.

On any given day I will receive catalogs and/or telephone sales calls from people who sell esoteric magazine subscriptions, hallway lighting, even telephone pole climbing gear...stuff I don't buy at all. For every one of these telemarketing calls, I receive about forty direct mail pieces.

In some cases, field salespeople visit me and pitch me on new office furniture, or something else I am not in the market for. Then, they call me back several times to see if I am ready to order something. I believe that I am pretty articulate, but, by my not being verbally abusive to the salesmen, they read it as a positive sign and continue to follow up. Even though I tell them I am not in the market for what they sell, they refuse to believe me.

A long time ago, somebody wrote a book, I think it was Zig Zigler, that said that the sale begins when the customer says no. Now, everybody in the selling game seems to take it as a personal challenge to turn every "no" into a "yes". If you have something that I need, this may be admirable.

If you have nothing I need, this is not only dumb salesmanship, but dumb sales management. Hasn't anybody ever heard of qualifying a prospect? If you want to make more money than ever before, you must manage your time and the time of your sales force and only spend time with true prospects instead of people who are simply too polite to throw you out.

The third reason *that people don't buy from you is that they don't trust you or your salespeople.*

I know you don't believe me, and they're often too embarrassed to tell you straight out, but it's true.

Maybe it isn't that they think you're a bunch of shameless, lying slimeballs who will say or do anything for a sale (although many prospects have just that opinion of salespeople); perhaps it is just that they don't have confidence in your company's recommendation...your professionalism. This is possible even in the medical profession. Let me illustrate.

Once, during a ski club trip to Park City, Utah, I was run down by another skier on the morning of the first day of my vacation. For the first time in thirty years of skiing, I found myself on the ski patrol toboggan headed for the medical shack. A doctor of the age and pre-shaving demeanor of Doogie Howser examined me. If you remember, *Doogie Howser, MD* was a TV show about a child prodigy who became a practicing MD coincident with his reaching puberty. The young physician examined me with the routine thoroughness that you would expect at a ski facility.

He then told me that I had torn a knee ligament and

immediate re-constructive surgery was a sensible way to go. If I waited, I might find that I did not need surgery. On the other hand, I might do even greater damage to a knee in a weakened condition.

The implication was that the surgery was the better way and the ski area surgeon was the most competent one to perform the task. To satisfy my fear, Dr. Doogie suggested I get a "second opinion" from his boss in Salt Lake City (an interesting sales strategy for a subsequent lesson, no?).

I told the doctor that I liked to buy my ski equipment near home, so I can bring it back if things don't work right. In my opinion, that formula works for surgical purchases as well. In spite of Doogie's best consultative sales effort, I took the next plane home to see the knee specialist at my local HMO. The bad news, according to my local surgeon, was that the young Park City doctor had correctly diagnosed that my anterior cruciate ligament indeed was gone. The good news, however, was that it was probably lost in a sporting mishap some two decades ago and I have functioned well without it all these years. My local specialist, also a skier, advised rest, mild physical therapy and no need for slicing and dicing.

I tell you this story because most of our prospects, yours and mine, view us with more skepticism than I viewed this young doctor. We sales types are viewed with skepticism because, more times than not, the advice given to buyers by sellers is just wrong.

Don't get on your high egotistical horse of professionalism. This has nothing to do with your own recommendations, but, rather, with the perception of buyers in general. Think about it. Do you always believe what highly-credentialed salesmen tell you? If I did, I would be walking now on a new plastic knee.

If you want to make more sales, you must recognize this unwillingness of many buyers to accept what your salespeople have offered based only on your own testimony. If you are to bridge this credibility chasm, you must arm your salespeople with ample references, third-party evidence to the competence of your recommendations. Do this and your closing ratio will climb significantly.

The fourth reason *that you fail to make the sale is that you haven't gotten your prospects to like you or your company.*

I mentioned that I receive a lot of sales calls. One cold call telemarketer actually said,

"HI! I SELL ACCOUNTING SERVICES. HAVE YOU FILED THIS
    YEAR'S TAX RETURN YET?"
"NO!" I GUSHED, "I WAS WAITING FOR A TOTAL STRANGER
    TO CALL. COME RIGHT OVER!"

Oh, brother! Does this guy actually expect to make a living this way? He might make a few sales, but he will not have a successful career no matter how friendly he sounds over the phone.

It is a mistaken belief by many in sales that likability and trust are solely the sales person's job. Image is a marketing function that includes sales training, collateral materials, and support for your local Little League team. That's why big companies give prospects copies of internal company newsletters that gush with wedding and birth announcements, and include photos of individual employees doing personal stuff.

The most successful selling mission meets the need to create an emotional bond between buyer and seller. The buyer has to care about you and he has to believe that you are nice enough to want to care about him.

The fifth reason *you don't get the order is because you fail to understand the internal politics of the prospect firm and create a true working rapport with all of the forces for change.*

Some people think that it is enough to train salespeople to target somebody called the "key decision maker", but this may not always be the top dog.

I recently heard of a case where the owner of a successful company told his CFO to give certain business to the owner's friend. Instead, the CFO gave the owner's friend's bid to the competition, along with the subsequent order.

When a salesman makes a deal with the number one decision-maker in a company, but the number one has a very egocentric, number two decision-maker at his side, you lose. Your deal is with number one, but your results are number two.

In fact, it can be documented that the company we are discussing consistently makes poor purchasing decisions, but the owner is unwilling to take a critical look at his CFO's performance. So, by not appealing to the CFO's ego, the seller and the owner have ended up in a true lose-lose situation.

In summary, the five areas that marketing can strengthen in order to improve your sales closing ratio are:

1) Uncover prospects who can afford what you sell,
2) Don't let salespeople waste time on prospects unless they have uncovered true needs for what you sell,
3) Build a company image of trust with references and other third party evidence,
4) Establish an image of corporate friendship and warmth, and
5) Train your sales team to understand the workings of corporate ego-politics.

Work on these points and watch your sales productivity improve without the need for a bigger marketing budget.

Creating an Artful Sales Story

For as long as there have been sales-people, those who have sold the most have relied less on artificial closing techniques and more on creating a strong emotional bond with their prospects through the sales story. Want to sell more? Then do this.

*B*y the time Ivan Lindgren had finished telling me about his company's relationship with AT&T, Ivan's relationship with his company, and what the trio of them could do for me, I would have signed just about anything. Ivan's title was Eastern Regional Manager of a major telecommunications value-added company and he was just great at his job. He was full of enthusiasm, knew what he was talking about and was a wonderful storyteller.

In less than an hour he had won me over, but not with a lot of fast talk and high pressure closing. Instead, he made a well-thought-out, methodical presentation that gave me opportunity to ask questions, voice my concerns, and identify the key benefits of dealing with his company.

To be sure, Ivan's selling skills are well honed, but the best part of the presentation was how smoothly he spun his tale of meeting client and dealer needs and the great partnership we would all come to cherish from this new alliance.

Most professional salespeople, like Ivan Lindgren, don't just pitch; they reveal their messages through the artful delivery of a sales story. Here's what they do:

1. Develop a narrative, or sales story, that has a beginning, middle and an end, just like any other story,
2. Organize, within that story, all the facts, relationships, benefits to be derived, and case histories into an interesting, informative flow of information,
3. Create a library of several compelling opening remarks to choose from, and
4. Build a *prima facie* case for dealing with them that starts with a firm foundation and then lays reason upon reason, until the conclusion is irrefutable: *Sign Here.*

Let's look at how you might do it now, and contrast that with a professional sales story. Remember that this is just a brief example upon which you would want to expand and embellish.

Old way: We're the Slick But Simple Software Company. Since 1974, we have been selling really slick software solutions for your business problems at very low cost by keeping things as simple as possible. We are better than the other guys because we care more. We really do. We really, really do. We care. Our clients say so. You can ask Fortune 100 International Corporation. We're also much more creative. Let's take a minute to analyze your needs and I'll give you a quote.

New way: We're the Slick But Simple Software Company. Our credo is a modification of the old KISS formula. We say, "Keep it slick, but simple." Interestingly, that motto was coined by the wife of our founder J. J. Slickworth when he first told her he wanted to start this firm back in 1974.

Back then, J. J. was senior development engineer for Bounce-back Aerospace Company. Aerospace had its ups and downs and J. J. thought he'd feel better about those mortgage payments if he built financial stability based on those good old American values he'd learned as a boy in Kansas. He shared his thoughts with the comptroller of the Fortune 100 International Corporation at a Rotary Club meeting one Tuesday night, and started his first project for Fortune 100 the very next week.

J. J. completed the project on time and under budget and Fortune 100 was very pleased with the results. They gave him three more projects and recommended him highly to Whatta Lotta Widgets and Holy Cow Chips that same year. That's when I came on board, along with Stephen Smith.

Our references were great and business was booming, but we hadn't yet set out our strategic course for the future. So, in 1976, we all sat down to dinner one night and decided that helping businesses manage costs was what we liked to do best and what we were best at. And that's what we've been specializing in ever since.

You can tailor a sales story to your business just as easily. To do this, first list your attributes, your market niche, your client references, and your chronological corporate history on paper. I know we're in the computer business, but, for some things, the screen does not substitute for several paper lists that you can tack up on the wall, or lay out on the floor, to get the big picture. Print to paper. Next, choose those items from each list that have the greatest impact, sound interesting to the casual listener and aren't too complicated to explain.

Be selective. Don't use everything. Concentrate on a friendly, even flow of information that will leave the listener with good feelings about your abilities for solving problems, your ethics, your references, and your willingness.

When you have written your first story draft, print it out and read it aloud in front of the bathroom mirror. It's amazing how many well-written scripts don't speak as well as they read. Easy to fix. Read it aloud to the mirror, again, and then to your next of kin.

Put the finished product aside for a few days and see if you don't find that your ad lib presentations start taking on the story mode all by themselves. Go back to your written story and review it for fresh thoughts and changes that have come from the week's field experiences.

After this, you probably will not have to ever look at this document again. You can, of course, but I'll bet that your selling story mellows and grows with each telling and you soon find yourself in greater control of the interview than ever before.

Welcome to the world of Ivan Lindgren.

Welcome to professional selling.

Soliciting Success: Part I

. . . . .

Top ten reasons I won't buy from you. No holds barred. I'm busy, your presentation is boring and you haven't a clue as to what turns me on, do you?

*W*ant to ring up sales from cold calls? Review my top ten phone-sales faux pas.

Here are my top ten reasons why I might not want to talk to you if you make your next cold call to my phone number (just like everybody else you are trying to get your foot in the door with).

If you study these reasons, you may overcome my objections. Then you can sell me and all of the other KDMs (key decision-makers) who have ignored you, hung up on you or otherwise shut you up. Here goes:

10. I am often too darned busy to actually listen to what you are saying.

The mail is backed up, and I need to spend time with three of my own salespeople who need advice, concessions, alternatives, solutions and other creative thinking so they can close deals.

Given the choice of spending my time to help you sell to me, or using that time to help my own salespeople sell our stuff to others, what should I do, talk to you? Don't fret. Just call back when I have more time.

9. You're too boring.

Think about it. You finally have the good fortune to get through to me, or to anybody, at a time when I am not three phone calls and two meetings behind schedule. So what do you say to turn me on? NOTHING.

The truth is, I do give most telemarketers more time than most people do and I even prompt the incompetent ones, which sometimes makes our staff fall down laughing. This morning, Lori DeFelice was downright hysterical listening to me coach an insurance salesman who had called, but had nothing to say.

SALESMAN: "MR. ROSENZWEIG, I'D LIKE TO COME BY AND INTRODUCE MYSELF."

ME: "WHY?"

SALESMAN: "I REPRESENT XXXXXX FINANCIAL SERVICES AND I WOULD JUST LIKE TO COME BY AND INTRODUCE MYSELF."

ME: "WE OWN A FINANCIAL SERVICES COMPANY (IT'S TRUE. MY WIFE RONNA, IN THE VERY NEXT OFFICE, MANAGES $75 MILLION). I MAY NOT BE YOUR BEST PROSPECT."

SALESMAN: "WELL, I'D LIKE TO COME BY AND INTRODUCE MYSELF ANYWAY."

ME: "WHY? WHAT CAN YOU DO FOR ME?"

SALESMAN: "I DON'T KNOW, BUT I'LL BE IN THE NEIGHBORHOOD."

ME: "YOU'LL BE IN THE NEIGHBORHOOD? I APPRECIATE YOUR PERSISTENCE. I REALLY DO. BUT, NOT TO PUT A FINE POINT ON IT, I DON'T HAVE A LOT OF TIME AND YOU REALLY NEED TO TELL ME WHAT'S IN IT FOR ME TO TAKE THE TIME TO MEET YOU." (AT THIS TIME, LORI, WHO HAS BEEN SITTING AT THE CONFERENCE TABLE IN MY OFFICE, IS ABOUT TO SPLIT A SEAM FROM LAUGHTER).

SALESMAN: "I CAN'T SAY WHAT'S IN IT FOR YOU, BUT I'D LIKE TO COME BY AND INTRODUCE MYSELF."

...And on it went, until I had to get on with the day. Face it. I gave him every opportunity to give me a reason to get that appointment, but he didn't. He blew it.

8. You sound too mechanical—not human, not warm.

You don't sound like someone I might want to get to know, nor anyone I would care about. If you want me to buy from you, you need to sound likable.

Don't think, for a minute, that telephone personality is something you are born with. It's not. Telephone personality is no more complicated than simply this: Imagine what your called party looks like and establish a conversation with him or her like you would with a stranger at a cocktail party.

If you take the time to visualize me as more than a phone number, I will feel it and I will not visualize you as someone sitting in front of an automated computer list dialing for dollars. It's the start of genuine communications.

7. I'm really the wrong guy for this meeting.

I may own the company, but I may NEVER get involved in the decision making for what you sell.

This is hard to convey to most salespeople, but it's true. I learned this very hard lesson the very hard way...not once, but twice, while training a new business associate who had great "business connections" four years ago.

First, we met with the owner of an enormous import business who turned to his CFO and said, "all things being equal, I want these boys to get the deal".

We didn't get the deal. I asked the CEO what went wrong. "My CFO wanted the other guy and I can't override him if I want to work with him." We knew the owner, but he was the wrong guy and we didn't have enough of a clue to consider working on the CFO.

The same thing happened one month later. Our new associate had a great list of friends who were happy to meet with us, but who would never step down to the decision-making process at our selling level.

6. I don't know if I can trust you.

I have had hundreds of people cold call me on the phone...and that's only this week. Who are these people? Why should I trust any of them? Why should I take the chance?

Nothing overcomes my fear like a good set of references. Testimonials impart credibility to give me comfort that you might be OK.

5. You're not offering enough free stuff.

What? You don't think I am so shallow that I would ignore everything that is really important about running a business to glom free trinkets?

Get real! Free stuff gets everybody's attention. I give away a great, but inexpensive six-inch ruler that measures floor plans in floor plan feet. They love them.

One year, Microsoft stole the show at COMDEX when they gave away thumb sized little white furry toys, which they called "Microsoft mice". Try this:

YOU:"LET ME BRING OVER ONE OF THESE VERY HANDY
    LETTER OPENERS AND TELL YOU ABOUT OUR WONDER-
    FUL NEW SOFTWARE."
ME:"OK."

4. You don't tell me anything that is new and informative.

New York City has three all news radio stations which keep us tuned in even on days when there is no news to listen to.

We have this great compulsion to be informed. Men suffer from this more than women, but women will listen, also, if they feel that they are learning something that isn't generally available. If you want to be really interesting to prospects, read the *Wall Street Journal* before each session on the phone.

3. You're not compelling.

There's no story line to your call. Consider how much more engrossing (and entertaining) you might be by simply telling me a story about your company, your customers, you, how you got into this business, etc.

The story has two benefits to both of us. It is a delivery vehicle for items four, six, eight and nine. Also, if the story is well rehearsed and entertaining, it keeps even the busiest Exec on the phone until you get him or her to agree to the appointment.

2. You're no fun when you're working.

No fun is depressing, and depressing phone calls are destined to fail. People who have fun on the job sound happy, creative and fun to be with. How can you hang up on a fun person?

In the spring of 1978, my company got a phone call one Wednesday at about 5:30 PM and there was no-body left to answer it but me. The caller worked for a hard-driving CEO who wanted her to get lots of bids to move their phone system from Manhattan to Stamford, CT.

"I HATE BIDS" I TOLD HER, TEN MINUTES INTO A VERY
    IRREVERENT CONVERSATION. "HOW CAN I RIP YOU OFF
    IF YOU COMPARE ME TO TWENTY OTHER GUYS?"
"AREN'T YOU EVER SERIOUS?" SHE LAUGHED.
"NEVER AFTER FIVE." I SAID. SO, WE MET AT HER OFFICE
    THE NEXT DAY (AT 5:30 PM, INCIDENTALLY).

We signed the deal and I got to move the phone system for Cahners Exposition, years before they became Cahners Publishing Company. Thus is the power of fun.

And finally, the number one reason why I may not want to talk to you when you make your next cold call to my phone number:

1. You don't sell anything that is useful to our company.

There is nothing as dumb in business as trying to get an appointment with someone without first qualifying them as a prospect for what you sell.

Think of the salesman in item nine, above. He neither knew, nor tried to learn if I could buy anything from him. If I had agreed to meet him, he might have simply wasted his time and mine. Now isn't that silly?

Before you make that next call, consider that for every ten people who sell on the phone, salesperson number ten makes more money than the other nine combined. If you want to be a "ten", learn how to avoid the mistakes of this top-ten list.

Soliciting Success: Part II

Top ten reasons why I am most willing to buy from you. The flip side: What the buyer really wants.

*L*ast lesson, I gave you my top ten reasons why I might not want to even talk to you, let alone buy what you sell. I gave you the reasons why you wouldn't get me from the telephone cold call to that face-to-face sales meeting you long for so.

If you learned from that lesson, congratulations! You are now one step closer to being one of those highly-prized, highly-paid sales professionals who sell me stuff that fill my supply room and empty my checkbook all the time.

Now, for the flip side, here are my all-time favorite top ten reasons that I am willing to give you the time of day, the shirt off my back and the money in my wallet.

Just for fun, let's buck the "Late Night" wisdom of 10, 9, 8, etc. and count forward instead of backward. You probably will appreciate knowing the most important reasons first (besides, it's been years since the Apollo moon walk and counting down is just not unique anymore). Once again, here goes:

1. You tell me what you sell right away and I need it.

Surprise, surprise. There are instances when people call me with information about something I have been longing to buy all along. If you have what I want, stop beating around the bush and come to the point. I really hate telemarketing managers who mislead their salespeople by encouraging them never to reveal that they are selling. Example:

> "HOW ARE YOU TODAY? I AM NOT TRYING TO SELL YOU ANYTHING, BUT..."

Do you really think that this crackerjack pitch is fooling me? DUH! It is much better to come right out with it and qualify me as your prospect like this:

> "WE SELL INTERNET ACCESS (SOFTWARE, LANS, ETC., WHATEVER). I HONESTLY DON'T KNOW IF YOU CAN BENEFIT FROM WHAT I SELL, BUT WE'LL BOTH KNOW IN ABOUT TWO MINUTES IF YOU WILL ANSWER THREE SIMPLE QUESTIONS, READY?"

Two minutes to find out if I will benefit? No B.S. about your not selling anything? Honesty? Great! I rarely turn down an honest caller, who respects my time, unless I am heading out the door for a meeting.

2. I need what you sell ASAP!

There are times when your timing is so perfect I can't believe it either. You call, honestly tell me what you sell and find out that I want what you sell right now...or I refer you to the guy who is gathering proposals even as we speak.

When this happens, forget about everyone else and concentrate on those of us who are hot to trot. When we buyers are itching to sign something, you'd think that we actually make your selling easy. Yet, unbelievably, I find that many of you who call me don't prioritize me to the top of your prospect list once I announce myself as a qualified prospect.

Recently, I went through hoops to find a quality copier salesman who had the service and features we needed in the price range I wanted to pay. Nobody wanted to make the effort to answer my questions.

Finally, one salesman found me and had the sense to drop everything and come right over. Result: we bought a machine on the spot. Telltale sign? We were expanding to new offices and everyone in town knew it.

In another case, I told an overhead projector salesman that my client needed one right away. He got back to us a week later, but, guess what...by then, someone else had already cashed the client's check because this salesman didn't have the time to drop his organized prospecting to visit an urgently qualified prospect.

Tons of marketing books have been written about prospecting to a targeted audience and many salespeople wear out their shoes pounding the pavement, or wear out their fingers "dialing for dollars" running through these lists when they should be paying attention to those they have already qualified, but don't.

If I need what you offer, your job is more than half done if you sell to me. If I become side tracked and I don't get back to you, call me with a follow up. If I am a qualified prospect, I want you to.

3. You have a really great product or service.

This may or may not be within your control. Not everybody sells great stuff. I don't care how brain-washed YOU are and how excited YOU get about your new, improved, Pentium clone for $26; it's not for ME. But when a salesman calls who really can deliver the goods without a lot of bull stepping...WOW! I can't wait to meet you. If you want to sell to me, sell great stuff and I'll listen.

4. I am the guy who has both the authority to say yes to you and the responsibility to say yes.

This IS a big point. You may have the right product for us and we may need that product, but I am not always the guy to buy it.

You know that many salespeople spend their whole careers looking for the so-called "key decision makers" but never learn the difference between those with authority and those with responsibility.

I have authority to buy everything, but I haven't the time, or desire, to become involved in every decision. Stop pestering those who have the power; instead, concentrate on those who want to be involved in the decision and you'll close more deals...I promise.

5. You've given me an immediate reason to trust you.

If you have a winning reputation and produce credible references, I will want to hear more. A strong brand name and a well-defined company image also help to establish this warm and fuzzy initial bond of trust.

When my salespeople prospect for new clients, we start by citing references. When prospects need convincing, we fax them written evidence and quickly call back for appointments. It works.

6. You're knowledgeable and informative.

I love listening to people who, obviously, can teach me things. If I feel that you have information, knowledge and creativity that you will freely share with me and I feel that I can learn from you, I not only will listen to you, I want to see you...more than once. Isn't that what kept Scheharazade going for so many nights (or was it her natural sales ability to tell a good story)?

7. You sound like fun.

If you are easy to listen to and are somebody I would like to get to know, I will listen. Your delivery should be upbeat and friendly. You voice should be energetic, but not so overwhelming that I get tired just listening to you.

8. You have free stuff for me.

Do you have an interesting, enticing deal, a promotion or special, an introductory rate, a free for a limited-time only offer, samples, etc. Do you want to give away something for nothing? Oh my, it's my lucky day. Sure I want one. Come on over.

But please, don't start off with a gift teaser that you later layer with so many qualifiers that I lose interest. We give out free gifts from time to time, and find them to be a great crowd-pleaser, just for seeing us.

No, no, not tacky calendars, cheap pens with your

name on them, dumb pins that end up in the trash. If you don't give something you would want for yourself, keep it away from me.

9. There is simple logic to using your product in our business.

Every now and then I get a call from somebody who is so organized in his or her thinking that I cannot help but see a clear and simple connection between what they sell and what I want, profits. They lead me through the sales process so quickly and effortlessly that I am entranced.

Most salespeople who call me are capable of this, but I think they just need more training and practice. Simple logic makes it easy for me to agree. Use it and you've won.

10. Price performance is easy to identify.

While we are on the subject of simple logic, how about finding an uncomplicated way to explain pricing without confusing me or putting me to sleep? I am so busy that I need to hear things that don't require a rocket science degree to understand.

To sum up, even though prospects like me are very busy, we all are on the lookout for any advantage to improve business. We will listen to you if we feel that you are straightforward and easily understood...like that panda who was recently in the news (as told to me by Ms. Katherine S. Naughton).

It seems that this panda had walked into a bar up in Boston, sat down and ordered a sandwich. Then he ate the sandwich, pulled out a gun and shot the waiter dead.

As the panda stood up to go, the bartender shouted,

"Hey! Where are you going? You just shot my waiter and you didn't pay for your sandwich!"

The panda yelled back at the bartender, "Hey man, I'm a PANDA! Look it up!"

The bartender opened his dictionary, which he always kept behind the bar for just such occasions, and he found the following definition for panda: "A tree dwelling marsupial of Asian origin, characterized by distinct black and white coloring. Eats shoots and leaves."

Now that's what I mean by straightforward and easily understood. The bartender nodded and the panda walked on out without having to pay for his lunch.

If that panda ever wants a sales job, I certainly have a desk for him.

Soliciting Success: Part III

. . . . .

Creative prospecting suggestions.
How to find more people who
will buy from you besides just me.

*T*o further leverage on the advice of my last two lessons, your burning question now surely must be "How do I identify those prospects currently in the market for what we sell so that when my sales force calls them, they are most receptive to us?"

Well, I've tried lots of ways to assure that our own sales force is always presenting to the right guys and gals and not wasting valuable time, and some of them actually work.

Of those we have experimented with, the three activities that work consistently best, for us, are:

1. Referrals and referrals of referrals,
2. Managed and tested promotions, and
3. Managed and tested cold-call lists.

Let's spend some time analyzing each of these.

Firstly, we all THINK we know how to generate referrals, but most of the resellers I come in contact with don't really exploit this most useful lead source to the max. Instead, most of us either rarely ask for leads, or, if we do, we stop right there, without exploiting the more fertile "referrals of referrals", which, as I will explain, is even a better source of business.

I once attended a seminar given by Chris Bruhl, Executive Director of SACIA - The Southwestern Area Commerce and Industry Association of Connecticut. The title of the seminar was "Association Networking - Making, Maintaining and Nurturing Relationships".

Chris is a charismatic speaker with an energetic smile and a friendly glint in his eye. He came to SACIA in 1990 after leading the Westchester, NY, Council for the Arts for the previous ten years. He knows about non-profit organizations and what makes them work...Networking relationships.

In only thirty minutes, Chris rolled out the most complete summary of how to do relationship marketing I have ever heard. His talk centered on how to reconcile an association's mission with your own, two agendas that sometimes diverge.

"Networking is the art of making, maintaining and nurturing RELATIONSHIPS, not just creating raw exposure," says Bruhl. "If you go to an association function and bounce from contact to contact like a pinball, you won't have much success, because simple exposure has no value. People die from exposure." he grins.

In fact, he proves his point with an example we're all familiar with. "Has anyone ever received a mailing from a total stranger that begins with "Dear Fellow Chamber of Commerce Member:..." A familiar chuckle is heard throughout the room.

"Did you instantly bond with the sender, or throw the mailing away?" The answer is self-evident.

This truth applies to all referral business, not just association referrals, and Chris suggests that we must focus on our own strategy as we bond with the collective mission of the organization. Many of us join organizations:

- **to provide visibility,**
- **to provide us with access to key players,**
- **to provide us with opportunities to demonstrate our capabilities, and**
- **to create initial relationships, which we call leads.**

Often, however, we miss the added opportunities of developing those relationships into lasting ones. Rubbing elbows with the CEO of a prospective customer at an altruistic fundraiser does not create enough of a bond to allow you to whip out your order pad.

The secret, according to Bruhl, is to build on that first relationship and avoid the temptation towards that premature transaction which will kill your chances later. Then, after you have become fast friends, you not only get the appointment, but you develop a friend who will tirelessly work through his own Rolodex, or PIM, to find you better prospects than you can get from the Yellow Pages.

I can say, without reservation, that this type of referral of referral prospecting results in more than 80% of the business that comes to us at Office Technology Consulting each year, so I believe in it.

By having all of your salespeople take the time to join with other business leaders in business and altruistic organizations, you all become familiar faces and improve your chances of being seen in a selling setting.

In addition to what Chris Bruhl has to say, I can think of two other benefits of participating in this kind of group therapy:

1. Consistent public exposure, this repetition, assists in establishing your image and building your brand credibility.
2. Community involvement gives you a chance to learn about your prospects, qualifying them so you can decide if you really want to deal with them, before you waste valuable sales engineering time.

The bottom line is that, pound for pound, dollar for dollar, hour for hour, nothing pays off as much as well-planned relationship building, strategically focused to generate referrals and referrals of referrals.

Secondly, in our top three, there is the marketing subject known as promotion and public relations (which some pros like to separate, but, for this discussion, we can keep them together). This is anything you do to get your name out to your potential market short of paid advertising, or getting yourself arrested. It includes newsletters, press releases, your internet website, listings on search engines like Yahoo, etc.

We concentrate on only two of those areas. Since we haven't the time to do everything, we concentrate on what has the biggest return for the investment of our limited time: website and press releases.

Let's talk about websites for a minute. During the past two years I have attended so many Internet seminars that I don't know how I have enough time left to answer my own Email. The quality of these programs varies greatly, but a few of them have been quite helpful. The most helpful thing I have learned is what I have always known (and wrote a column about four years ago): Keep it simple, stupid.

What I've learned is that, once again, strategically focusing on what you want to accomplish is the key to success in promoting what you do. Take our own website phoneguru.com. For starters, it's not big, not flashy, not high tech and it doesn't use Java. In fact, some have said that it's downright hokey...but I did keep it simple and it does meet all of our objectives for a website.

Want to know what those objectives are? There are two:

1. **Expand my business.**
2. **Make more money.**

Did "phoneuguru.com" do that? Yes, in the following ways:

1. It doesn't take a lot of time to manage, so our overhead is nil.
2. It creates a warm, friendly image - prospects have become customers and customers have become friends.
3. You can surf the entire site in three minutes, the time it takes other sites just to load home page graphics.

Everyone who comes gets the simple message.

4. We have special pages, not on the menu, for special prospects, customers and friends. If I want to make you feel special, all I have to do is refer you to phoneguru.com/you.htm. There I will have your picture on the net, a flattering bio of you, a list of the top ten jokes that have come in from our Email chain-letter joke factory, etc.

(By the way, we have received about 1,150 jokes from clients, so far, and another hundred that are so tasteless that even I am too put off to post them. If you want access, you have to send two new jokes via Email).

If you are a developer, or VAR, or any other type of business-to-business enterprise, you don't have to spend a fortune on the net to make it work for you. Start simply by posting free and valuable reference material for easy down-loading. People love to be helped and they really, really love free stuff. They remember it too. Add a few success stories and references and you can have a website that adds value to your product and brand.

Alternatively, since many of our own prospects are not yet web savvy, we have opted for releasing all that infor-mation to the local business press.

I have had a few lunches with the editor of our local paper. I like him a lot and he likes me, resulting in about one to two published pieces per month - a nice, consistent flow about us. This promotion effort helps by creating a positive, growth image. People know of us when we call, helping to make the sale.

Finally, for this lesson, I'd like to take some time to review the attributes of purchased lists and how they can help you... or not.

Using mailing/phone lists, the truth be told, is the coldest, hardest way to prospect, with the lowest success rate. That being said, it often has to be done, because, even this least likable means of finding customers works, and can lead to success until you develop enough leads from the referral method.

I've researched two companies that provide a flexible means of targeting your calls: American Business Lists, Omaha, NE, and IMarket Inc., Waltham, MA. There are others coming to market all the time and they will, I am sure, do an equally adequate job for you. For now, let's do a head-to-head shootout between these two.

Each provides CD-ROM products with about the same 10 million or so business records, but they verify them differently. ABL claims that they call every name twice a year (although I can't recall ever hearing from them). IMarket is associated with D&B and uses their cleaned database.

The two companies meter usage and sell by the name, phone number, etc., resulting in a final cost to you that is roughly equivalent to buying printed lists, except you have them on media and can reprint, remail and otherwise reuse them without further charge.

We have found from spot checking that the ABL list tends, for us, to be more accurate and provides several key employees at each company, versus a less accurate list from IMarket.

On the other hand, the IMarket people are formerly Lotus developers who have built an intuitive front end that is much easier to use with a much more refined targeting ability. With IMarket, we feel that we get better targeting, but with somewhat less accuracy.

Of course, the Chris Bruhls of the world can be of great assistance, here, as well. In our own Stamford, CT, SACIA maintains an accurate list of 8,000 executives in 3,000 companies in our county. The association sells the list at a surprisingly nominal cost and they provide paper, media and even mailing services.

Whether you sell by geographical region or nationally by vertical niche, working through an association that encompasses your market may prove to be a more accurate and more cost-effective way to go.

Just remember Chris's admonition, however, about mass mailing or phoning without effective relationship building: "Simple exposure has no value. People die of exposure."

When You're Too Darned Lazy to Sell

• • • • •

Five steps to creating a canvassing-free sales environment. Let's face it, pounding the pavement is not always the best use of your time...especially if there's a better way.

*M*ost of my career I have been just too darned lazy to sell. You know what I mean. That feeling of sales procrastination is overpowering when the mountains are calling me to go skiing in the winter, or to go hiking in the warmer months.

For you, it might be the siren call of your fishing boat, your golf clubs, a good book that you couldn't put down until 2:00 AM, or late night reruns of the O.J. trial. Whatever causes our laziness, up until now there has only been one piece of unkindly sales managerial advice echoed throughout the selling world: GET BACK TO WORK, YOU BUM!

Well, enough of that salesman abuse (and self abuse, if you work for yourself). It's time for you to try a paradigm shift to what former President George Bush might have called a kinder, gentler sales model...one that has given me a quality of life one only finds on Baywatch.

In order to reach this beach ball bliss, I have rediscovered five steps to marketing success that virtually eliminate the drudgery of cold-call prospecting. That's right. This is a program that will allow you to downsize your telemarketing department, for instance, and still make more money next year than you have ever earned before...without all of those management headaches that salespeople create for you.

I came upon this program, interestingly enough, by reading back issues of magazines and other sales and marketing materials, including over 100 of my own marketing columns. But, enough about me (as the old saying goes), here are the five steps I now use, the reasons behind each of them and how I am using them to build a canvassing-free sales environment that has filled our pipeline like never before.

Step one
Research your market to identify a product vacuum and identify what you have that people will buy right now.

This sounds simplistic, but don't skip over this part. It is as important as it gets. Isn't this, after all, how Fed Ex got its start?

I have noticed, from my research of past articles, that many of us become so smitten by our own ideas of what our customers need that we often fail to offer them what THEY think they need.

A dozen, or so, years ago, for example, I was convinced that Microrim's RBase would take over the database world simply because it was the easiest to learn and the fastest to run. I was younger then and I wasn't experienced enough to take the time to ask the market if easier and faster were enough to create a market dominance. So I was quite surprised when it didn't and we lost more than a fair amount of time, training effort and money trying to convince people otherwise.

Back then, we sold well enough, but we didn't take enough time to listen to what the market was really telling us about ourselves. Whenever I would meet with other business owners, they would say something like:

"YOU DO SOMETHING WITH OFFICE CABLING, DON'T YOU?
BOY IS OUR CABLING SYSTEM A MESS."
"NO." I WOULD REPLY. "WE ARE IN THE TOTAL SYSTEMS
INTEGRATION BUSINESS. BLAH, BLAH, BLAH."

More recently, by comparison, we applied step one of this five-step plan and revisited our marketplace to ask them what intrinsic core competence they thought we had that they actually needed, knew they needed and wanted someone to provide.

Now, this is an unremarkable concept that has been noted in these pages from time to time, but, like in the Kellogg's Corn Flakes commercial, I had to "taste it again for the very first time".

What I "tasted" was that whenever people move their

offices, or enlarge them, or upgrade their infrastructure, or even downsize their staff, they need somebody to advise them as to how best to modify their cable infrastructure. Evidently, everyone had thought that we were the best outfit to handle that chore, but, until performing our recent research in step one, I never realized that this could be a full-blown market niche for us. You might find the same kind of ready-made niche in your own business.

In our case, clients found that cable providers were too close to the selling process to plan it from the buyer's perspective. Meanwhile, architects and space planners were too far removed from the technical training to keep pace with changes in the business. This revelation brought me to step two.

Step two
Create a new product or service offering from the vacuum identified in step one.

Some may say that this is the most important step (and who am I who argue?). But, for me, it is also the easiest. Why? Because, I have always found that reaching the destination is never as hard once you have mapped a destination to go to.

In this case, we determined, after all these years, that our advice in planning cable infrastructure not only saves construction costs today, and saves reconstruction costs tomorrow, but that clients recognize our ability to meet that need and are anxious for our help.

So, to complete step two, we decided to promote that infrastructure competence. But how should we get the word out? Remember, we are "lazy" salesmen, after all. This leads nicely to step three.

Step three
Find a ready-made sales army who are already well trained and who will benefit from carrying your flag into battle for you along with their own.

I remember reading about how the post-World War I German Army was to be limited to a small force, so it would no longer be a threat to the rest of Europe. Never faulted for their lack of efficiency, Germany spent the next decade building a small army of field officers who all would be capable of commanding troops.

The key to an effective army, they reasoned, was not to have large numbers of soldiers, but to have the most number of effective leaders who could be counted on to accomplish many varied missions when required.

From that example, once we determined what our new marketing thrust would be, we considered how best to get our message out. We turned our attention to who else might benefit from promoting our work to their clients. Two groups emerged: Architects and Commercial Realtors.

These two groups are involved with most corporate infrastructure changes, are thought of as highly professional and benefit themselves when they can identify solutions to the client problems we identified in step one. Introducing us to their clients becomes a big win-win.

Our decision was, therefore, not to canvass potential clients, but to create strategic alliances with our new army of professionals who:

1. Already had the clients we want,
2. Recognized the client's needs and desire for our help, and

3. Would enhance their relationships with their clients by calling on us to meet those client needs.

Make no mistake about it. These professionals have their own businesses to run and they are not going to stop what they are doing to sell our services. In order for them to be of greater use to their clients and to us, we have to make it very easy for them. This led to step four.

Step four
Provide your army with weapons to win your battles.

This is a tough one. If you are too lazy to sell and you want others to do that for you, you must give them weapons. Yet, you must also recognize that this is neither a paid army, nor one of loyal countrymen fighting for an ideal, nor one that is full time, nor one that even thinks about you very often.

In our case, we wanted something that could do the selling job for us, was easy enough for our army to carry around, would not require changing established habits and would be both unobtrusive and all-encompassing at the same time.

By process of elimination, we finalized on a series of 8 1/2 X 11 brochures, tri-folded down to envelope size, which meets all of the stated criteria. They are easy to read, are easy to carry and promote professionalism. "Boring" is not always a bad look if you don't want to be thought of as sales-y to start with.

We compensate for small and easy to carry by using a more expensive four-color look, even though we are targeting a very small audience and don't require large print runs. It's amazing how much more receptive people are to color graphics. Also, I put my photo on the back panel.

I have found that, like Frank Perdue, Chrysler's Lee Iococca and Wendy's Dave Thomas, no matter how ugly you are, people who have never met you are willing to accept you if they know what you look like. Fidelity Funds got a big boost from investors when they pulled Peter Lynch out of retirement to pitch the company on TV. Interestingly, we test mailed one hundred of these brochures to a very targeted army capable of quadrupling our business if we weren't careful. This generated twenty responses, which set the stage for our final step, step five:

Step five
An army travels on its stomach. Feed it well...and often.

Every respondent was offered lunch. Everyone who accepted lunch was offered another lunch. Every meeting paid for itself in new business referrals of significant size.

Two members of our new army became clients themselves. One member of our new army brought us a large and famous international financial services company as a client.

We only lunch with senior officers or partners, movers and shakers. Yet these lunches are not four-hour, four-thousand calorie orgies. Senior people are trying to cut down on both. They are productive meetings and they are very much fun to do.

So, my five steps for building your business are:

Step 1. Research your market. Identify the product vacuum,

Step 2. Create a new offering to fill that vacuum,

Step 3. Find a ready sales army to carry your flag into battle,

Step 4. Provide this army with weapons that will win, and

Step 5. An army travels on its stomach. Feed it well... and often.

This is the perfect way to build a growing business... especially when you are just too darned lazy to sell.

It's Who You Know
· · · · ·

The secret to great marketing is not brains or beauty. It's building spheres of influence with professionals who serve your prospective clients. How to build a steady stream of referrals from those who can best provide them to you.

*H*ard driving under the influence…"It's not what you know, but who you know." "What goes around comes around." "One hand washes the other." To most of us, this is part of the bread and butter world known as "sphere of influence marketing".

Creating spheres of influence is just like farming and nobody you know who has ever climbed the sales ladder to the top, did so without cultivating and then harvesting sources of information, leads and contacts from their own private garden. You think the Donald made, and lost, and made his fortunes on his intellect?

When I first left New York Telephone and went out on my own, one of the first really successful telecommunications salesmen I'd ever met turned out to be a neighbor named Len London. Len never thought of himself as an intellect and he was the first to admit that he didn't really understand how technical apparatus worked. He just sold the stuff.

Nevertheless, Len rose through the ranks to become President of his company. He never stopped being that company's star salesman and ran it profitably for years until, with its parent company, it was merged into another business and he was able to cash out.

Len didn't know a bit from a byte and didn't want to know. "All I can tell you," he would say, "is that this system works well, can do what you want and we have a great team of service people if you should need them. End of technical discussion. Sign here."

So, if he couldn't discuss the merits of his leading edge technical products, what was Len's great sales success secret? Simply put, it was spheres of influence. Len had dozens of them.

For over 15 years that I knew him, it seems that I was not alone. In fact, it sometimes appeared that there wasn't anyone in the New York Metropolitan Tri-state area who was connected with telecommunications who wasn't part of Lenny's wide web. They called him. They joked with him. They trusted him and they bought from him over and over again.

Near the end of his tenure, I visited Len one day at his office and was surprised to find that, in spite of the fact that he was running almost a $20 million division, he had no personal secretary, no Internet, not even a computer...and his desk was clean and neat.

On it there were photos of his beloved family, a phone and a Rolodex. These weren't many items with which one could run a business, but, as a working environment, they were more valuable to Len than the client database of Heidi Fleise, The Hollywood Madam, could be in the hands of Geraldo Rivera.

The photo of a typical American family (Lenny, Leslie, Lisa and Larry London...and the dog Lolli) gave Len the motivation for success. The phone gave him the means and the manual Rolodex, filled with business cards and personal notations, gave him sufficient sphere of influence opportunity to fill his day, and fill his company's work schedule.

The last time my desk looked that neat was July 5, 1973, the day I started my first company. The only materials on my desk that day were two pieces of paper. One was a schedule of income projections for my first quarter. It read: Sales = $0.00

The second schedule was a single page with a single entry representing my only client, Garcia Corporation. Garcia needed a strategic plan to communicate among its offices in California, Colorado, New Jersey, Austria, France and Italy. In 1973, this was no easy task.

Getting such a large first client project was the catalyst that allowed me to quit my job and hang out my shingle. It had been a lead that was given to me by my neighbor Len London. He told me that it wasn't a job that he could do, that I owed him nothing.

There was no quid for this quo except that I do a great job and not embarrass him...and if ever there were a client that he might serve, he only hoped that I would provide him with an opportunity to bid fairly. I did and he provided some of my clients with extremely competitive proposals and quality service.

This is the obvious result we all seek in sphere of influence marketing, but why does it work so well for people like Len and fail so miserably for many of us?

There are several reasons, but one that is high on the list is focus. In this regard, I have the focus of the cobbler who can never find his glasses and whose kids run around barefoot because there's always something more important for him to do than sole their shoes. There are a dozen or two projects on my desk at any one time, not counting the ones on my desk at home.

As I write this, we are harvesting a bumper crop from our sphere of influence seeds that were planted during the past four years. A couple of large projects that were bid over a year ago through spheres of influence have finally come in and individuals that I have befriended without recourse, in the Len London tradition, are now responding, unsolicited, with new opportunities.

In addition, business plans drawn up during the first quarter to improve long distance telephone service for the clientele of our spheres of influence are now generating consulting sales. We, also, have received several significant inquiries, regarding our supplemental business plan, to provide our spheres of influence with pre-paid telephone calling cards for affinity groups, fund raising and potential resale.

I know that this seems to belie the need for focus, but, on reflection, I know that, if we were to be more focused in serializing our opportunities, I am sure that we could plan out our activities with less of the roller coaster effect on our revenue stream that makes each month so exciting.

If my own rock and roll sphere of influence marketing style brings me some satisfactory level of success, what the more focused style does for my wife is nothing short of spectacular. Ronna manages portfolios for small groups and individuals and her growth in assets to almost $75 million in just a few years is due to focusing in on her spheres of influence and through targeted public speaking.

She specializes in helping women with significant assets who are recently divorced, or widowed, and managing pension accounts of small professional groups. Her clients are more interested in not losing what they have than they are in quadrupling their money over night.

Accountants and attorneys have become aware of her successes with these clients and they now approach her with requests for private interviews with their own parents, sisters, cousins, etc. What better sphere of influence can there be than somebody whose mother is a reference?

At a "Women in Business" seminar not too long ago, Ronna was the speaker hit of the afternoon, not by selling, but, instead, by giving great advice on how not to lose money to Wall Street sharks. This prompted several investment group leaders to ask her to speak at their own functions, combining the spheres of influence concept with new hubs and spokes where each spoke then leads to a new sphere.

Way back in 1969, Milton Weiner, one of the top

agency managers for The Equitable Life Assurance Company, told me that successful life insurance salesmen never depend on one form of lead generation. They canvass on the phone. They canvass in person. They choke our mailboxes with offers for free copies of the world atlas in exchange for our sending back the year we were born (don't you just love it?).

But the really big producers, according to Milt, one of the biggest producers of them all, develop intricate webs of spheres of influence. They work on these webs constantly to uncover the best opportunities for large financial gain. Like spiders, that diligently extend, repair and manage their webs every day, they never go hungry. Many of these salespeople have no technical training, but they learned about the multiplier effects of web marketing long before the world wide internet came on the scene.

Speaking of hungry, there's one more great tip that came from Milt. If you want to be a major player in any business, never waste a lunch hour eating alone. Share the time with your spheres of influence and you will always keep busy.

Keeping the Message Simple

The KISS formula has served us well. Here's how it can do the same for you. Examples of complex companies who have succeeded with simple messages and how to apply the concept at home.

*K*eep Your Marketing Message Simple! One of the most useful and fundamental communications lessons that has been repeated to me over the years, ever since my earliest days of formal business training, is the fabled, famous, and fabulous "KISS" formula.

In my college marketing class we were told "Keep It Simple, Stupid!" When I entered my three-month sales-training orientation at New York Telephone way back in 1968, it was a more refined "Keep It Short and Simple."

New York Telephone didn't want us recruits to hear negative words like stupid. In Army OCS we were given a variation of KISS, KIFSS, which wasn't quite as short and simple, but left its firm, indelible training mark with a greater sense of, uh, military bearing.

However we choose to preface it, the fact is that simple messages have the greatest impact. That is why concept slogans like "Intel Inside" are so successful.

Think about how the major players in today's highly successful technology sector apply the KISS formula. Microsoft simplifies its message in its definitive product names: Word, Office, At Work, Excel. These are all KISS names that don't require you to think too much to figure out what the products are about. (Who knows, they might have used the name WordPerfect, but, alas, it was taken.)

Symantec has the best-selling Windows®-based fax program of all time. Symantec's product lets you send faxes right from your current application. It lets your PC receive faxes in the background while you run other software. It imports fax phone lists from your Personal Information Manager. It comes with 200 different and creative cover pages. It allows you to set up a broadcast fax newsletter.

Symantec's fax program is so sophisticated that, if most of us owned it, we would probably need six pages to explain what a great sales and marketing tool this software is. So how does Symantec convey the message of all these wonderful features?

It chooses to do so with the name of its software, another great KISS name: WinFax Pro. Can these guys market a message, or what? Famous four-letter marketing words like easy, fast, safe, and love (as in you'll love it), are fine for selling TV dinners, but for the rest of us they should be supplemented to great advantage with a well-chosen word picture that describes what you sell.

If your product or service is not already a household word in your vertical niche market, rather than rely on words like fast and easy, what you really need to convey is a word that tells what. WinFax Pro tells "what", and it blows away all competition. End of story.

Which brings us to your message. Are you able to simplify your message down to a couple of words? Do you? You should, but how? Here's a simple four-step formula for simplifying your marketing message and defining your market position.

Step one
Think of all the things you do and sell as accommodations to meet customer demands, and then work up a more narrowly-defined, focused list of those things you prefer to sell to make money.

When you get right down to it, you probably offer a lot more products and services than you want to, but you have to, in order to meet certain customer expectations.

This is fine, but let's face it. Unless you're a distributor like Wal-Mart or Costco, you don't really want to promote everything you sell, do you? I know I don't. Loss leaders are not a part of the value-added service niche that we are comfortable with, although dozens of Internet companies are willing to lose money to buy market share in the hopes of selling, not profitable products, but their own stock on Wall Street. I've been reading the red-ink quarterly financials of the latest of these short-term wonders.

My strategic marketing plan is to send my price conscious customers over to those websites to buy everything they sell below my cost. I figure that if the website is able to sustain this abuse, my customers will love me for the advice. And if the website keeps losing money and folds, well, hey, I've lost another competitor.

So, to summarize step one in the KISS process: simplify your own view of your products and services by determining specifically what it is that you make your money from, and establish or reaffirm your priorities to concentrate on that defined market.

Step two
Determine who your competition is and what makes him/her better.

Or at least try to determine why other people buy from him and not from you (Lesson One, "Why Prospects Don't Buy", should be of use in this exercise).

How does a fresh competitive analysis assist you in simplifying your message and improve your chance of success? First, it's a reality check to determine if you have chosen the right niche to dominate, or if you merely are suffering the after-effects of second-hand smoke from Cheech and Chong's cigarettes. (If you don't understand this, ask your folks and I guess I am older than I think).

Second, how can you even consider communicating a competitive positioning message unless and until you can verbalize what you are competing against?

Step three

Now, let's discuss what you bring to the marketplace that's newer, cheaper, stronger, better tasting, less filling, fat-free, or otherwise truly unique.

Under no circumstances are you allowed to say that you "care more" than the competition, or that you are "more service oriented". Everybody says that.

At Office Technology, we have two profitable market niches. We resell long distance service from one of the national carriers, and we integrate voice-data solutions. Neither market solution is proprietary to us, but we have identified where we are most competitive.

In technology we seem to have an edge because we know how to set up a system that's so user friendly, it doesn't cause our customers' customers to hang up on them in disgust. In long distance, we simply sell the same national carrier's calls at five cents per minute, coast-to-coast.

We are not all things to all people, but we are all things to some people, sort of like Rush Limbaugh or the Hollywood Madam. You probably fit the same description. If you take the time to write down what you do that is all things to some people, you can take it all the way to the bank.

Step four
You've defined your focus, decided where you can't beat the competition, and determined where you can beat them cold. Now tie it up in a neat verbal bundle.

Remember, the point of all this is not to see how cute you can write; that's my job.

Instead, just try to communicate simply and directly what you do and what you want the reader to do (like call you). Most importantly, don't forget to test your message on the unsuspecting to see if what they read is the same as what you think you wrote.

A winning message is one that can be read on Monday and recalled on Tuesday or, dare we hope it, Wednesday. I test my material out on friends, relatives and the guy who owns the local diner - people not in the business.

I figure that if those outside the business can easily understand what I'm talking about without explanation, then I won't have to worry that my message is too obscure or cryptic. That's the heart and soul of the KISS formula.

It's by keeping things simple to say, simple to read, simple to understand and, especially, simple to recall in a couple of days that we multiply our chances to sell. Simple messages are easiest to remember. And if customers remember our messages, they are much more likely to remember to call us. Now that's worth a KISS and maybe even a hug.

How to Lose a Sale in One Easy Lesson

After winning the toughest sales, don't let the easy ones get away. Case studies of sales that we should have, would have, could have...but didn't.

*H*ow many tough sales do you fight tooth and nail for while perfectly-good, easy-to-close, lay-down deals go by the boards, completely lost in the shuffle, because you couldn't get your act together enough to make a timely proposal?

Here are several true cases from both my business and personal life that should make us all sit up and take notice and, perhaps, give more thought to submitting our proposals, making our deliveries, and solving our customer service problems in a more timely manner. I'll start with one that I am really reminded of every time I look at the missing comma in my checkbook balance.

At our company, we know and love our clients and they know and love us. We are most happy when we are able to provide existing clients with extra cost savings from products that fit well with our services. One of the services we like to sell to that existing client base is discounted telephone long distance.

Our carrier only charges between three and six cents per minute, which is dirt-cheap and the quality is as good as it gets. Sometimes, however, the process of providing a quotation breaks down and nobody wins.

This case history involves a company that spends over a quarter of a million dollars each year to call Europe and the Far East. At that volume, they were already getting a pretty good deal, as you can imagine. But the client said they would drop that existing good deal for ours, if we would submit a reasonable bid.

The Vice President of Sales of a long distance company we were representing really wanted the job, but their international rates were not quite competitive enough. Everyone at this carrier offered to be a lip-service team player and all agreed that they would do some sharp pencil figuring on those international rates.

I telephoned our carrier of choice several times, faxed them the client's phone bills, not once, but twice, and re-minded them several times during a six-week period, looking for the competitive pricing proposal they said they earnestly wanted to submit.

Unfortunately, almost two months of my nagging went by before they could get their "pencil sharpener" working and, because their back office couldn't get it together in a timely fashion, somebody else signed a three-year $700,000 deal with my client. Ouch!

It turned out that the competition got the deal at the same price that we would have charged had we received our proposal a little sooner. This is not an isolated case. I'll bet that you can tell me about a few of your own...deals that wanted to be closed, but that you didn't meet them half way. Here's another interesting object lesson.

We are not a major user/reseller of shrink-wrapped software, so we still have to shop around for the best prices. When one of the biggest, fastest-growing stocking distributors started hammering us with direct mail promos and telemarketing calls, we decided to source several UNIX items from them for a new client installation.

The big distributor did not have the best pricing, but they agreed to meet the competition's price for this order. However, when the software package arrived, they had back-ordered licensing for five stations.

Have you ever told your customer that you could install only fifteen workstations now and the other five when the rest of the software arrives? You know that you can't install a system without all of the station software and/or licensing, so I called the sales rep and asked him if he would substitute a full 5-user package with disks and docs for the backordered license package and that I would pay the full package price just to meet the customer requirement.

The full package substitution was shipped, but at a higher price than one originally negotiated, plus additional shipping and a $5.00 minimum order charge to cap it off. So, the inconvenience of not getting what I wanted in a timely manner, compounded by the paperwork needed for a supplemental order, was further aggravated by our being nickeled and dimed after the fact by a company that doesn't bother to skimp on costs when it sends me about a hundred bucks worth of advertising mail each month.

This kind of nuisance charging, when a substitute order is an accommodation from me to the distributor, who didn't have the required stock, well, that's just plain rude, isn't it?

Adding further insult to injury, we had to make three phone calls and stay on hold several times only to find that our request for justice had a only a chance of being approved IF the sales manager, who wouldn't come to the phone, would sign off on the adjustment. We gave up and hung up... for good.

Large stocking distributors were then growing at such a terrific clip that they might have been tempted to forsake the smaller customers who are their bread and butter in leaner times. But remember too, the number one maxim on Wall Street and in real estate: Everyone's a genius in an up market.

Whatever goes up, eventually comes down. If you are too unkind to too many people, they won't be there when you need them and all of your promotional mailings and telemarketing efforts can be shot down by a single lack of civility.

Here's a personal example of how no-brainer sales are lost all the time. In this case, I was the prospect who was dying to buy something. Have you ever had such a prospect who was real hot to trot when you met him, but turned ice cold after you sent him the proposal? Now that I have become more of a conspicuous consumer, I have begun to understand the process.

Several years ago, I had just gotten married, moved into a new home and decided that I would like to follow up on all those ads encouraging us to change over to gas heat.

I called the gas company and got a nice young man on the phone who said that he would have to send a request to engineering to determine how much they would charge me to bring the gas pipe to my door from the street.

"FINE," I SAID, "WHEN WILL YOU CALL?"

"DON'T KNOW!" HE REPLIED.

"ONCE IT GETS TO ENGINEERING, THERE'S NO
     TELLING...COULD BE A COUPLE OF WEEKS. WE'LL LET
     YOU KNOW."

So, having a couple of weeks on my hands, I called a few plumbing contractors to get pricing on the furnace and installation. Three contractors responded, but, interesting enough, they all said the same thing:

"I'LL WORK UP A QUOTE AND GET BACK TO YOU."

Several weeks passed and, of the three contractors and one gas company, do you know how many people got back to me? Right. NONE! You know how much money I spent converting my new home to gas? Right. NONE!

Why? Well, while I had time on my hands from not having a contract to sign, I decided to contact the really expensive electric company to find out why they were really that non-competitive.

Turned out that they weren't so bad after all and that the amortization of a new system would take most of the next decade. So my new wife and I decided to keep the ten grand and apply it to a bunch of ski trips. My needs hadn't changed, but my impulse power couldn't last a whole month.

Speaking of skiing, Tom Dwyer, who was the terrific manager of the Pedigree Ski Shop in my home town of Stamford at the same time I was learning about the quick response of the gas company, gave me a great lesson in how to make an ordinary customer into a loyal and profitable one by being both timely and helpful. Tom is the ultimate value-added reseller specializing in adding value to sporting goods sales.

For over a year, I had suffered with a pair of ill-fitting ski boots that had turned me from a mogul meister into the agony of the feet. When Tom found out, he lost no time in getting the boot maker to give me a new pair, which was a major feat, but he did not stop there. Although there was no cash profit in it, he spent hours making sure that the boot fit and I was happy. Since then, I have convinced the better part of my ski club that there is no better boot fitter than Tom and no better ski shop than Pedigree...and my wife and daughter have been helping raise the sales curve at Tom's store.

Tom Dwyer proved, again, that timely, quality responsiveness is one of the best marketing strategies we can employ. There is a lot that this retailer can teach a telephone carrier, a gas utility and an overgrown software distributor. Tom's lesson and our lesson for today: if you can't get it right the first time, make getting it right the second time your first order of business.

Shut Up and Listen
. . . . .

**Your presentation can never compete
with your prospect's internal one.
Here's the specific knowledge you need
to butt in on that silent conversation
your prospect is having with himself.**

I have great respect and deference for any organization that uses the word "billions" in its everyday routine accounting (companies like McDonalds come to mind). When a management type from such a company asks me when I am free for lunch, I usually answer, "Right now".

So I had lunch the other day with one of my long-term readers who happens to be a senior marketing manager for one of our industry's "largest" companies and, during the two hours of marketing philosophy and diet cokes, my host got me to thinking about how difficult it is to empathize successfully with our prospects.

Often we talk about customer empathy, seeing things from his or her perspective, but do we do this successfully? Really? My luncheon partner took the opportunity to praise my monthly marketing column. Then he challenged me to upgrade his newest twenty-slide presentation that detailed the value-added intricacies that should have made doing business with his company a slam-dunk no-brainer.

The presentation discussed working knowledge of vertical market niches, value-added engineering and staging, unlimited technical support, and a logistics system that would support hundreds of customer sites simultaneously. Nestled in the presentation were allusions to lowering overall costs and lots of warm, fuzzy, partnering terms.

I was impressed at the quantity of details and concepts that were presented, but what was it that was missing here that would compel...I say COMPEL the customer to stop everything and sign up? The missing ingredient was empathy with the prospect's true feelings, wishes and needs. I'm sure that you think you understand empathy, but I'll bet that you don't have the same understanding of that term that I do.

To me, empathy is the full understanding of BOTH conversations the prospect is having during your presentation. It is very important that you involve yourself in both of them. You know, of course, that none of us ever has only one conversation at a time.

You know how we all carry on these secondary, private conversations with ourselves at the same time that we are having outward conversations with other people. Even as you are reading this, you are now having thoughts about other, totally unrelated, things aren't you? It's OK, because while I was writing this, I was visualizing my ski trip in Colorado that would begin in two more days.

Think about it. When you talk to your spouse, child, friend, business associate, etc., you have two conversations. Your primary conversation is the one where you physically speak and listen to the other person. The secondary conversation is the separate, but simultaneous, one you have with yourself that may or may not have anything to do with the primary one. The secondary conversation you have with yourself either:

1. Interprets information from the primary conversation your are having (e.g. - She said that I would save us money with this new purchasing program, but was she just being overly optimistic? How does the Value-Added component actually translate to the bottom line? She can't possibly believe I can save all this, can she?),

2. Filters through only the information you really care about and disregards the rest (e.g. - blah, blah, blah...and your markup is $90,000 on each network order...blah, blah...You will only have to devote two days a week for two lessons), or

3. Removes you from the primary conversation or even replaces it entirely (e.g.- I wonder when I can politely end this meeting and turn on the latest ball scores? I wonder if those overnight packages went out to the West Coast? Does this guy really make a living in sales?).

Putting empathy into your sales presentation doesn't necessarily have to mean anything more than your being able to understand and control the prospect's secondary conversation.

Building such empathy and control into your presentation by using industry-specific knowledge is more of a marketing strategy than a sales tactic because it can be implemented corporate wide, at the systems and training level, rather than by salespeople in the heat of the moment.

As a systemic matter, your enterprise must train salespeople to understand specific issues, needs, unique operating difficulties and peculiarities of each specific vertical and then provide your sales teams with the specific ammunition to address and control those secondary conversations.

Getting back to the slide show of my friend with the billions, I suggested that he shelve all of his slides and replace it with an informal, simple discussion. I say simple, but one that would direct both of the prospect's conversations by empathizing with the prospect's known goals. Let's try it, shall we?

"MR. PROSPECT, YOUR GOAL IS TO OPERATE MORE PROFIT-ABLY AND SO THERE ARE THREE WAYS YOU CAN CUT COSTS."

"FIRSTLY, YOU CAN BUY CHEAPER BY BEING A BETTER SHOPPER. IF YOU SEE COMPONENTS FOR LESS MONEY, YOU CAN BUY A FEW AND TRY THEM OUT. IF THEY WORK, YOU CAN BUY MORE. THIS TAKES EFFORT, BUT PRODUCES SAVINGS."

"SECONDLY, YOU CAN SAVE MONEY BY BUYING LESS, MAKING DO WITH WHAT YOU'VE GOT, OR STRETCHING OUT THE PURCHASES INTO THE NEXT QUARTER. I'M SURE

YOU'VE DONE IT WHEN THE CURRENT QUARTER'S
BUDGET WAS OVER THE LIMIT. SOME DEPARTMENT
HEADS GRUMBLE, BUT, HEY, IT WORKS."
"THIRDLY, YOU CAN BUY SMARTER. YOU CAN IDENTIFY
EXACTLY WHAT IT IS IN SO CALLED VALUE-ADDED
PURCHASES THAT ADDS VALUE TO YOUR BUSINESS, YOU
CAN QUANTIFY THE TRUE ADDED VALUE TO YOU AND
SIMPLY DISREGARD THE REST…"

These three points are not new to those of us in
marketing and sales, nor to most prospects, but isn't it re-
freshing for prospects to hear them from the other side?
The fact is, your prospect's secondary conversation includes
these very items, so by addressing them head on and early
on you can begin to influence that other conversation, too.
Now for the second part.

"HERE ARE FOUR SPECIFIC WAYS THAT WE AT OUR BIG
DISTRIBUTING:
FIRSTLY, WE PROVIDE UNIT COSTS ON PAR WITH THE LOWEST
COMPETITORS. WE MAY NOT BE THE LOWEST PRICED
FOR EVERY PRODUCT, BUT, ON AVERAGE, OUR PRICING
IS AT THE LOWER END…"

The prospect's second conversation doesn't have to
wonder at what your general language about savings was all
about. Now he can stop daydreaming about an intangible.

"SECONDLY, OUR SNAP-TO-IT SHOPPING FORMULA GUAR-
ANTEES PRICING AND AVAILABILITY. THIS IS A SPECIFIC
VALUE-ADDED SERVICE DESIGNED TO REMOVE THE NEED
FOR YOU TO HIRE AND MAINTAIN A PARTS ORDERING
DEPARTMENT. HOW MUCH DOES IT COST YOU TO
STAFF THIS DEPARTMENT NOW?…"

By pointing out the specific cost advantages to your value-added benefits, the prospect's second conversation is now concerned with actually computing the amount of annual savings that will accrue to his own firm from his being able to do with two less bodies, less desks, lights, computers, FICA...all of the costs.

"THIRDLY, OUR VIRTUALSHIP PROGRAM CAN AGGREGATE, STAGE, BUILD, TEST, PACK AND DROP SHIP TO AS MANY AS 300 SITES PER ORDER FOR YOU. THIS VALUE-ADDED SERVICE PROVIDES YOU WITH A VIRTUAL WAREHOUSE, LIGHT MANUFACTURING, TESTING AND SHIPPING FACILITY AT NO ADDITIONAL CHARGE. CAN YOU ESTIMATE HOW MUCH THAT WILL SAVE YOU?"

Again, his second track has been given tasks relating your empathetic message, so he hasn't any room for other thoughts. In fact, he is so involved with parallel processing your new data, he may be about to display an out-of-memory message. You're using specifics to gain control.

"FOURTHLY, HERE ARE FOUR REFERENCES OF CUSTOMERS WHO ATTEST THAT OUR TESTING PROGRAM HAS VIRTUALLY ELIMINATED RMA's (RETURN MAINTENANCE AUTHORIZATION). THIS HAS SAVED ONE CUSTOMER OVER $40,000 LAST YEAR. HOW MUCH DOES IT COST YOU TO PROCESS RETURNS EACH YEAR?"

Most likely, he doesn't know the answer to this question, but his second track should be busy working it all out.

You might recognize a universally accepted sales method, that of involving the prospect by asking qualifying and trial closing questions. Of course, that is a means of empathizing. In addition, though, you need to be aware of the subliminal activity that is constantly around us.

Recently, I witnessed the art of a mentalist that illustrates the power we can wield over this secondary conversation. Even though I wrote this lesson months ago, let me use that art to read your mind in the future, as it were. I will discover three thoughts that you don't even have yet...The thoughts for all of you who are now reading this (editors, too).

Please follow along with a pencil and write in the margin on a page that doesn't have my picture on it (so that I can't read what you write). Choose a number from one to seven and write it down. Great. Now double that number. Now add 8 for a new total. Can you handle this so far, or do you need a calculator? Fine.

Now take the new total and divide it by two. Got it? Good. Subtract the original number to get a new result. Now to make it interesting, let's see if we can change the number to a letter of the alphabet. If the number is 1, call it an A. If the number is 2, call it B. If 3, call it C, etc. Got a letter? Fine. Now think of a country that starts with the letter you have chosen. Good.

Now, for variety, try to think of an animal that begins with the very NEXT letter of the alphabet that follows the first letter of the country you chose. Finally, think of the color of that animal.

You are thinking of a country, an animal and a color. Got it? You have done your job very well. Now let's see if I can figure out, from the past, what you thinking today. Hmmmm.

That's odd. I wonder why you would choose grey elephants. They don't live anywhere near Denmark.

You think there's anything to this empathy stuff?

My luncheon host agreed with this new slant on the money-benefit empathy issue and he wondered if he should scrap his formal slides. Not a chance, I thought. These details will be critical for the follow-up meetings to put flesh on the bones, so to speak, and to provide the thorough understanding that we need our strategic partners to have.

Mining Gold in Your Own Sandbox

· · · · ·

How would you like a fresh new list of prospects you hadn't thought of before? Two tests that will surprise you and three ways to build new business from existing relationships.

*H*ow would you like a fresh new list of prospects you never thought of before? How would you like them to be fully qualified local prospects who need what you sell and are pre-sold on your ability to deliver what they want and need?

There is such a list for most of you and I'll prove it to you. By the end of this lesson, you are going to say, "Of course," and you'll slap yourself in the forehead like the guy in the V-8® commercial. But first, a little two-part test.

Here is Part A. Pick up a roster from one of the clubs you belong to: ski club, sailing club, bowling league, any one will do for the moment.

Now run your pencil down the list and check off each name where you think you know what the guy or gal does for a living. Check twice if you are 100% certain. This test will uncover two amazing points.

Amazing Point #1: Very few of your friends on your list have been checked twice. Those who were checked twice are sales types, traditional employees of large companies, school teachers, or other government workers. Except for the sales types as lead sources, they are probably not prospects. The friends who have been checked only once also are not in the majority. They could be business people who may be prospects, but you never learned enough about them to make it worth while.

Amazing Point #2: The greatest number of people you know and associate with through social organizations have not been checked even once. This proves metaphorical, since your failure to check them on your list means you failed to check them out in real life. Not only does this mean that you don't know what they do, it means that they probably don't know what you do, either.

After all, if you haven't taken the time to know them professionally, why would they take the time to learn about you? The fact is, most people you know don't know what you do for a living...even your relatives.

"Oh, no! Not my relatives!" Yup. Let's prove it with Test Part B. Pick up the phone and call your Aunt Bea or Uncle Sid. Don't wait until you see them. Family visits heap tangents upon tangents and you'll soon forget the test. Besides, it could be months before you see the family again.

Once, I posed the following question to my sister, an aunt, an uncle, a cousin and a nephew, all whom I am quite close to: Tell me what you think I do for a living?

Here are the answers:

- Something in computers.
- Something in telephones.
- You work for the phone company.
- You are a writer (close).
- You are a business advisor (real close, but vague).
- I guess I never gave it much thought (honest and perfect).

If you are honest, you will learn that the people who know you, and are willing to give you the benefit of the doubt, often do not hire you simply because they do not know how you can help them. Conversely, by the way, those very same people in whom you can place the most trust and confidence do not sell to you for the same reasons. They don't know your needs and you don't know their strengths.

It is not an easy task to bridge this communications canyon and educate the scores of potential prospects who know and love you without being the boring leech of the party. How many times have I been cornered by the canapés, day dreaming of altering a favorite bumper sticker to "Guns Don't Kill People - I Do!"? No, captive audiences do not yield good prospects.

Instead, here are three ways to communicate:

1. Become genuinely interested in what other people do.

Don't just ask people what they do so you can tell them your own story...and certainly do not interview people. Nothing is more crass. Do learn to become interested in others for the fun of it, even if they do not end up as potential prospects. Genuine heartfelt interest is recognized, appreciated and responded to in kind. It is a habit worth developing.

2. Place descriptive "booster ads" in club newsletters, if appropriate, or have your firm sponsor club events.

It is very appropriate to provide complete product and service descriptions at sponsored events. While this often results in a higher cost per reader than commercial publications, don't forget that you are targeting a very specific group of people who know you, but need to be educated as to what you can do for them.

3. Take the time to ask people, "Do you know what we do? Do you know of all the services/products we provide?"

This works very well on phone calls, at luncheons, during lulls in casual conversation. I am continually surprised that long-time clients in one area, telecommunications, for instance, have no idea that we do a lot of work in custom programming, or that we sell laptops, etc.

If you see an opportunity to do business and there is not enough profit in it to satisfy you, pass it by. If you have the skill and you can negotiate enough profit to make it worth while, do the deal and stop worrying about how much everyone else is making. You'll make a better living in the long run...and you'll feel better, too.

Lesson 11... *Mining Gold in your Own Sandbox*

Failure to communicate your range of abilities to those you know is a big mistake. Failure to recognize how little you and your acquaintances know about each other is a bigger one. By addressing this, you uncover new opportunities through existing contacts, reduce the uphill credibility battle of cold calling to strangers and even find comfortable new ways to meet your own sourcing requirements.

The Fine Art of Using References

· · · · ·

Are you as good as you say? Who else says so? How to get references and use them to increase sales.

*E*ven though you may be really good at what you do, there's often a great gap between what you think you are capable of and what you can convince your prospects that you are capable of. This credibility gap is illustrated by a story about a young man who has just completed medical school.

It's graduation day and the young man's relatives, including his aging, immigrant grandmother, are sharing in the joy of his successful completion of his medical studies from a very fine school.

"WELL, GRANDMA," THE YOUNG GRADUATE SAYS AS HE
HUGS THE OLDEST OF THE GROUP, "TODAY I AM A
DOCTOR."

The kind and patient old woman, proud, but stooped with age, looks up at her tall and handsome grandchild and smiles with love. There is some skepticism in her voice that this child could, in fact, be accepted to such a responsible role in society.

"SONNY," SHE SAYS, "TO YOU, WHO KNOWS HOW HARD
YOU'VE WORKED THROUGH ALL OF THESE YEARS AT
SCHOOL, YOU'RE A DOCTOR. TO ME, WHO LOVES YOU
AND WANTS TO BELIEVE IN YOU, YOU'RE A DOCTOR.
BUT, TELL ME, TO A REAL DOCTOR, ARE YOU A
DOCTOR?"

How many times have you walked away from a perfect presentation thinking "this one's in the bag", only to find out later that you didn't get the job? What went wrong? Did the prospect hear everything you said? Did he remember it all?

Chances are, he did, but just didn't believe that you were the "doctor" you claimed to be. No, he didn't think you were a fraud and he accepted your thesis that you thought enough of yourself that you could complete the project you bid on. But he wasn't convinced that someone better able to judge than you thought so, too. In other words, no matter how honest, and creative, and responsive you are, you didn't make sufficient use of qualified references to tell your story for you.

To raise the comfort factor among your prospects, there are several ways you can generate references that will attest to your abilities to do your job and help you to land more sales. In fact, if you DO do good work, you're doing yourself and your prospects a disservice if you don't generate evidence of your success.

The most common and most popular is the letter of reference. It is relatively easy to come by, but many of us fail to ask for it because by the time we have earned it, the job is winding down and we are thinking about the next one.

Too bad, because asking for a reference letter serves three purposes:

1. It gets your client to thinking proactively about you, great for additional work.
2. It uncovers hidden problems in the job while there's still time to do something about it. Reluctance to provide a written reference brings this out.
3. It produces a reference letter that can be used in your selling efforts. A great, low-cost marketing tool.

A second kind of evidence is to get your present clients to recommend you to new prospects. I recently discussed my plans for the coming year with the president of a national convention center for whom we have been working on a major expansion. I asked him who he thought would make a good prospect for us next year and if he could be called on as a reference. This project has been very successful, but this client proved even more generous than I would have hoped for and offered to write a personal letter to the heads of ten major convention centers, extolling our virtues and pointing out the benefits of retaining us.

Back in New York, I told this story to the president of a major real estate firm, also a client. "That's a great idea," he said. "I'll write a letter to the ten largest real estate firms in New York and tell them how helpful you've been to us."

In only two conversations, I was given an enormous amount of publicity and marketing assistance. Now, I don't have to tell prospects how great I can be for them. Others, far more credible than me, tell them how great I have already been.

Those who are new to business sometimes ask how they can break out of the Catch 22 situation of not having any references to get enough jobs to create references. There are more choices for references than client testimonials. While not as strong as "He did a terrific job for me and really solved my problem", references addressing your abilities, financial strength, business longevity and integrity can prove useful, too.

Take a reference like this: "In the 14 years that I have known John Smith, I have found him to be honest, trustworthy and diligent. He won't take a job he can't handle." This would be a very helpful selling tool if it were written by your banker or the dean of your college. It would be less effective, however, if the best source for this type of comment was Uncle Mike.

Of course, references, in the long run, are only as good as you are and truly great references must be earned over the course of time. This means that in order to rely on references to grow your business, you must return to old-fashioned values of quality, patience, care and empathy for your clients.

While quick-buck artists end up facing bank failures, real estate venture collapses and other days of reckoning, those of us who might have been beginning to question our steadfast adherence to ethical principles and practices eventually see clearly that our hard work and honest efforts are worth more than just the respect we receive from the guy in the shaving mirror... although, that's very important, too.

If you do good work, your clients appreciate it. They want you to be successful because they want quality to be rewarded. Also, they want you to still be around the next time they need you. Include them in your marketing plans by asking them for letters of reference and for referrals to others they know in business who will respect their opinions and who will benefit from your expertise.

The Art of the Deal

· · · · ·

What's in it for me? What's in it for you? These questions are the key to every deal. How often have you heard, "It's only a good deal if both parties are satisfied"? Mutual satisfaction is raised to a fine art. Here's how to bring color to your own negotiating palette.

*H*ow often have you heard the statement, "It's only a good deal, if both parties are satisfied?" Or maybe you've heard the lawyer's corollary, "It's only a good contract when each party claims it gives too much to the other guy".

While both examples are commonplace, it may not be that it is so much the actual terms of any agreement, but rather the psychological perceptions of the agreement holders that are requisite to a satisfactory arrangement. Those who fit the first statement and look, primarily, to the accomplishment of their own satisfaction tend to get what they're after. Those who fit the example of the second are so consumed with what the other side is getting, they lose sight of their own goals and must fail.

Must fail? Did I say must fail? Yes, I did, and here's why. I think of a successful business person as one who never forgets the two fundamental points of any business deal: "What's in it for me?" and "What's in it for you?" The first part makes the deal worth doing to you, while the second helps you to sell it.

Notice the order here. What's in it for ME comes first. To be successful in negotiations, or any business activity, we have to be able to set practical priorities for the use of our limited time, don't we? Shouldn't we know enough about what we're getting out of any deal to be able to give it the attention it deserves, (if, indeed, it deserves any attention at all)?

On the other hand, once we've established what it is we want out of a deal, our next step is not to figure out how much more to squeeze out of the other side so that we can gloat, but to determine how to make it as attractive as possible to the other party, since it takes two, as they say, to tango.

Making a deal attractive to the other party without reducing its attractiveness to you below your minimum expectations is what Donald Trump used to refer to as the "Art of the Deal", back when people were hanging on the Donald's every word the first time before his fall from grace and subsequent rise again. I never stopped hanging on to a lot of his words.

Unfortunately, too many of us are more concerned with what the other guy is getting and how much better he may do than we will. I recently told a story at a dinner party about earning a $100,000 fee for engineering a solution that will earn a client five times that, a half million dollars, each and every year from now on.

The dinner guest two seats to my left said, "Too bad you didn't know sooner. You could have charged them two hundred thousand." Easy for him to say. The truth is, I am very happy with the fee, the work and the client. I would be happy with the arrangement if the client earned a million a year from my work. I went into this deal with expectations which were met and I got what I wanted.

Recently, a programmer friend complained about a job he had subcontracted from a larger marketing-oriented company. He had agreed to take 75% of the billing when he thought the job would only bring in $5,000 based on hourly work. As programming jobs go, this one grew to over $45,000. "My extra work brought the other company an extra $10,000 for the same sale," my friend complained.

Did he complain that he was given the opportunity to earn almost $38,000 with absolutely no marketing or administrative overhead or development time to charge off? He was concerned with the wrong end of "what's in it for you" thinking. He agonized over someone else's surprise good fortune, instead of showing them how good he could be for them.

If his psychology had led him to "what's in it for me" thinking, he would have been so ecstatic over his $38,000 windfall that he would have pressed the larger company for more work at the same rate and the additional projects would have propelled him to his best year ever. Instead, he told them that, henceforth, he would require a higher percentage of billing and didn't get another job from them.

Now I'm not saying that you shouldn't cut yourself a sweetheart deal if you can. Athletes and entertainers do it all the time. But, if you want star status, you had better have an irresistible and irreplaceable top act. Bobby Valentine, Manager of the New York Mets, once explained to a Chamber of Commerce gathering in his old home town of Stamford, CT, how he came to own seven Bobby Valentine restaurants. "My contract was up as a baseball player just about when free agency came into being, so I thought I'd try it out."

You know what happened when he tried to play financial hardball? Yup! None of the major league teams hired him to play baseball after he declared his free agency, so he had to change occupations and he went into the restaurant business. True story.

Bobby had figured that there was more in it for "them" then there should be, and he KNEW that he was both irresistible and irreplaceable. He is, but back then none of the owners knew it for many years.

Even when our government finally conceded that the last recession was upon us, there was a substantial living to be made for all those who didn't run for cover, but, who, instead, kept "What's in it for me," and "What's in it for you," in perspective. No flat economy ever meant a tailspin for everyone. Most Americans still have jobs and most companies still make money. There are those who have expertise in areas without prospects and those with clients who would rather not redevelop new processes and products from scratch. There is room for joint ventures that benefit everyone, even the clients.

Direct Mail that Really Works

· · · · ·

Did your last sales letter get lost? Or was it simply tossed? Short, simple and easy-to-apply secrets to getting your next mailing read.

*I*sn't it amazing how well the Postal Service seems to prioritize mail? Outgoing checks reach our suppliers in 24 hours. Incoming checks take weeks and weeks to reach us. Sales letters, "must have gotten lost in the mail. What did you say your name was?"

The sad truth is, unless you're attempting commerce in midtown New York City (or a few other well-documented theaters of conflict), delivery of your checks and your letters doesn't take more than a day or two, and the actual loss of first class items are rare indeed. Regrettably, your letters aren't being LOST; they're being TOSSED.

Quit suffering the paltry 2% industry average for sales letter response. To create successful direct marketing letters that get read, be concise, be complete and be sure you ask a closing question. Make your points in dramatic, quick moves, like a quarterback, not in slow, tedious ones, like a mail sorter.

Here is a direct mail piece that I recently test targeted to 100 prospects. I'll tell you the results in a minute:

MEMORANDUM

TO: (each individual)
FROM: Stan Rosenzweig
DATE: xx/xx/xx
SUBJECT: Local Success

We're Thrilled!
We've just helped the ABC Company reach these four objectives:

- Improve customer service and staff performance,
- Assure system reliability,
- Lower operating costs,
- Minimize risk associated with change.

In collaboration with Mr. John Smith, ABC Co.'s General Manager, here is what we did:

VOICE

- Improved client member services,
- Doubled incoming call handling with new phone system,
- Reduced front desk attendant staffing requirements,

- Reduced clerical staffing requirements at departments, and
- Provided more benefits, while reducing budgeted costs.

DATA
- Negotiated large refund from existing dealers,
- Planned more efficient workflow throughout network,
- Expanded network at HALF of original budget,
- Established better data reporting, and
- Improved daily performance and ongoing reliability.

We are now looking for new business opportunities to improve client efficiency, assure working reliability and reduce operating costs in all telephone and computer services. Companies in the process of relocating present a unique opportunity, but we work with in-place clients too.

I would appreciate your referrals. Give me a call for more information or just to pass on a good lead.

Thanks.

Each piece was mail-merge customized, that is, it was individually addressed and it went in a separately addressed envelope (no mailing labels, please). We sent it out on our best letterhead stock, yet I chose the MEMORANDUM format because I believe that ordinary business letters are so routine to most of us that we have ceased to read through them. Memos, on the other hand, at least for now, are less frequently received and are more apt to create some kind of unique interest and response.

In fact, within three days, I received six phone responses and two good leads that I might not have gotten if I had not sent out this written "Hey, I'm still here" memory jogger. Our staff followed up with telephone calls during the next two weeks and received three more leads. These memos and subsequent phone calls let our contacts know that we were thinking of them, reinforced what it is we do and moved them to action.

Past experience tells me that at least 20 of these 100 memos will create order activity within two months. In other words, a planned, complete, well-positioned communiqué, with scheduled follow up will result in a 20% favorable response.

In addition, the memo has gone through recycling and its contents, without the memo header, will be appended to every other letter we send out for six weeks.

A response of 20%? Baloney, you say. Everyone knows that direct mail only yields a 2% response and that a phone follow up increases that number to 6%. True, enough. Those are the AVERAGE numbers for an average letter with an average phone call. But a few things make this letter anything but average. Take a closer look at the breadth of this memo, how it is constructed, and what it contains. Notice that it:

- Positions us in a special way - as benefit producers, not commodity sellers. We sell brainpower, not hard goods;
- Tells a rapid-fire success story, so the reader can identify;

- Provides a good reference, with a name that can be called;
- Reinforces all of our strengths - a good reminder;
- Provides the reader with a checklist, or shopping list, of items to consider for today and tomorrow; and
- Asks, unabashedly, for new business or a referral.

The memo tells what we do, how we do it, and how you can benefit from it, all on a single, easy-to-read page. Notice that it does not waste the reader's time with an opening that isn't relevant, nor does it drag on for pages and pages, to be read only by those who aren't busy enough to be prospects, or those who are very, very lonely. This piece is brief but complete...and that's why it gets such good results.

By comparison, I received a detailed two-page letter, recently, that went on for four full paragraphs before I learned that the writer provided customized PC enclosures to the trade. All of the preceding and subsequent information was of great interest to him and would have sounded OK to me in a face-to-face discussion, but I might never have gotten to the point of the letter before routing it to the round file if it hadn't been a slow mail day.

Before you send out an individual letter or a 10,000-piece mailing, ask yourself:

- What do I want to accomplish?
- What do I want to communicate?
- Does this do it?
- If it were sent to me, would I read all of this letter?

Every marketing letter should be written based on some well-defined marketing premise. For this one, I wanted to position us more as a company that is known for reliability, performance and risk avoidance, rather than the usual stuff about bits and bytes.

I believe that whatever market niche, vertical, or segment you are in, you probably need to position yourselves the same way, because, what resellers don't do is sell hardware or software. Sears sells hardware. Egghead sells software. Resellers improve businesses. That's the Value we provide. That's the V in VAR.

If you can get these thoughts across with more excitement and in fewer words than the AVERAGE direct mail piece, you will have better direct marketing results.

Doing Business with Clients Who Hate You

· · · · ·

Let's face it. Not everyone loves you. Can you still get them to give you money? Three steps to getting even your most dissatisfied customers to increase their orders.

*W*ays to get more business from customers who hate you. Elsewhere in this manual, I have discussed when to turn down a project and how, and when and why you should cancel a project in progress when it doesn't improve either your short-term or long-term business. The flip side of this is that most of us would rather learn how to increase business with existing relationships rather than eliminate it.

Positive actions do help us maintain a general positive mental attitude. Besides, these days we really need the work. Reseller Management Editor Tom Farre, in April 1991, noted that getting a new customer costs six times more than keeping an old one. He went on to reveal that 96% of unhappy customers never tell you so, sulk in silence, and that two-thirds of them would gladly buy from you again if you would solve their problems.

Great research! In two or three paragraphs Tom told me that I have a great new prospecting list to work from:

- One that is exclusively mine
- One that I don't have to pay a list company for
- One that is accurate and up to date
- One that provides me with a direct line to the key decision makers
- One where those key decision makers actually want to talk to ME
- One where I have an estimated closing ratio of 2:1
- One where my closing ratio will yield over 300% of the original sale

This is incredible. Look at how much wealth you can earn from the 96% of your unhappiest customers - those silent sufferers. It almost pays to tick off EVERYBODY and reap the resulting windfall bonanza. Well, almost!

Do you get one complaint per month (you should be so lucky, right?)? If only 4% of these troubled souls actually complain, then 12 complaints per year means that there are 24 times 12, or 288 non-complainers with problems...excellent buying prospects who need to be contacted right away. Truth be told, the bigger we get, the more we tend to let things fall through the cracks and for those of you who are biggest and most successful, those cracks tend to become small chasms and before you know it you're Evel Kneivel trying to negotiate the Grand Canyon.

In order to turn potential disasters into more business, and to use successes to gain new referrals, do the following:

1. Send each existing customer a "report card" and ask former New York City Mayor Ed Koch's famous question, "How'm I doin'?"

Ask a series of specific questions such as: Are you satisfied with us? What can we do to make things better? What specific problem can we help you with? Who can you recommend us to?

2. Don't expect everyone to drop everything to answer. Give them a reason to.

Enclose a free gift and offer an even better one for respondents. That's TWO gifts, folks. Let them know that you think their thoughts have value to you. Remember, a new account costs six times more to sell than this one costs to keep.

3. All marketing people know that repetition is the cornerstone of marketing success.

One mailing does not a campaign make, so stock up on those "report cards" and include them with your invoices, your monthly statements, your newsletter (you DO send out a newsletter, don't you?), and even to your future prospects as evidence that you will be interested in their reactions long after you clinch the sale and spend the deposit money. It's a nice touch, I think.

A few years ago, I identified a few business relationships with fellow VARs that had "gone south" in recent years. I decided to test drive the thesis of this lesson, along with the premise that I first put forth in *Reseller Management Magazine* back in October 1989, when I wrote, "there's still gold in the golden rule".

I made an appointment to meet with the one of the offended customers at the customer's office at 6:00 PM, after the phones stopped making everyone crazy; Miller® time, as it were. We discussed old times, new times, hard times, the *New York Times*, and the times of our lives.

Ultimately, I learned that we had done dozens of good things for this customer over the years, but that somewhere along the way I had dropped a quip that was perceived to be strongly offensive and cavalier. Now you all know that there is nothing in my sense of humor that could ever be considered offensive and cavalier any more than you could make that case about talk show host Howard Stern who was fired by a major network for disparaging a certain minority group for its sexual preferences.

Well, I was so shocked at this revelation that it was immediately apparent to the customer that I was totally ignorant of the offense. Sentence was commuted, I was forgiven and we opened a new negotiations direction that will be worth not six times the original order, as suggested by Editor Farre, but HUNDREDS of times the value of the original order. The customer became more than a customer of ours, but a VAR/dealer promoting our services to over 2,400 of its own customers.

The other side of the coin is reflected in a situation where one of our software suppliers allowed one of its former employees (who had been our support person) to approach a large prospect that he had met during a joint presentation to automate the prospect's sales force. It was a meeting that we had set up. We thought that the software firm did not act fairly and we cried foul, of course.

The president of the software firm, possibly under pressure to increase sales by the venture firm that had just become an investor, not only refused to acknowledge our claim of "foul play", but refused to even discuss our complaint with us directly. His position was that the prospect could make up its own mind as to who to deal with.

Now this was our prospect that we brought this software company in to meet, so we weren't too thrilled about this lack of loyalty. What did we do? Nothing. Nothing at all. We didn't go after the prospect any more. We stopped selling the product to other prospects, as well. We see this as a necessary survival tactic to market only where we feel we can rely on future returns for present efforts.

We don't hate these guys, but we no longer trust them. We are now among the 96% who don't complain, but simply stop buying. We could be resold, but it would not be time effective for us to convince the software people that they need to act more honorably.

So, the first way to get new business from existing customers who are less than friendly is to find those customers who are most unhappy with you, identify their reasons for dissatisfaction, solve the problems and become great heroes who live to serve and who should be given more work, which we have already established as being considerable.

Secondly, by narrowing your dissatisfied customers down to a precious few (let's face it, nobody's perfect), and by certifying that almost all of your customer base now loves you dearly, you can demand, and receive, a great number of quality referrals.

Nothing will make your sales department happier than a cornucopia of referrals from satisfied customers...and notice that these are very special referrals, too. Referrals are always appreciated by the sales force, but when they have been generated by a successful service-based effort, rather than by salesmen, they are positively manna from heaven.

Service-generated repeat business and referrals are both better marketing concepts because an existing customer has an appreciation of your integrity, as well as your sincerity, and will go out of his way to pay you on time and tell everyone about your good work...not bad for someone who started off hating you.

Making Educational Seminars Sell for You

· · · · ·

Seminars are an ideal way to educate your prospects and win them as customers. If I owned a deli, I would pass out samples of Swiss cheese. Information can be offered as samples the same way.

(This lesson is a reprint of a column that I wrote in June 1993. I think that there is a good sales lesson here that I would like to share with you as it was originally written. I hope you agree and find it useful.)

*I*f you'd like to see how hundreds of your peers use seminars to market their products and services, attend a seminar in your industry at one of America's great convention centers.

I won't be envious with you, because I am one of those hundreds who will be trying my best to impress the heck out of you. In fact, joy of joys, I am lucky (or skillful) enough to be on lots of programs.

On Thursday, I will be part of a panel discussion on how to write an effective RFP (Request For Proposal). On Friday, I will join with several modem manufacturers to talk about how the future of high-speed data communications will change the business world as we know it.

As professionals, why do so many of us go the seminar route to get our message out? After all, there is preparation time and the expenditure of creative energies to prepare a satisfying show. In addition, nobody ever pays good money to the presenters.

There are lots of reasons to do this, but here are a few of the better ones:

- Qualified decision-makers will listen to us for up to an hour or more. Between 300 and 600 attend my PC EXPO seminars and a seminar is a great ice breaker and rapport builder,
- We get to show off our extensive knowledge and creativity and we establish an air of deference and respect, and
- Out-of-pocket costs are minimal. Cost per qualified lead is so low it's hardly worth mentioning.

Let me tell you about two of the professionals with whom I have shared the limelight, and why they've chosen to appear, coming from all over the country at their own expense.

One of them is Mark Bennett, Director of Marketing and Development for Pine Island Software, a vertical marketer of email and messaging systems. When Mark phoned to invite me to be on his panel, "Modems 101", I asked him why he chose to lead seminars at PC EXPO and other events year after year.

"YOU GET A LOT OF SERIOUS BUYERS AT THESE THINGS", MARK TOLD ME. "LAST YEAR, SEVERAL PEOPLE FROM THE AUDIENCE CAME UP TO SEE ME AFTER THE PROGRAM AND ASKED ABOUT OUR PRODUCTS...EVEN THOUGH THE PROGRAM HAD NOTHING TO DO WITH WHAT WE SELL."

Mark understands the crux of seminar selling. You teach lots of good, useful stuff, prove how truly valuable you can be and make them want more than you can possibly fit into an hour and a half.

Barbara Miller, Manager of Product Technical Support for Hayes Microcomputer Products, Inc., understands this, too. She also knows that even the most technically macho among us shamefully cast our eyes to our shoes and cower at the thought of signing on to a bulletin board or information service...and herein lies her opportunity.

Barbara won't be talking about Hayes products, but, instead, will provide quick, simple answers to allay our fears of wasting countless, frustrating hours trying to get these marvelous little electronic critters, modems, to do their jobs.

So, if you come to PC EXPO this year, don't expect to see Mark, me, or anyone else on the program, taking advantage of our captive audiences to make any kind of sales pitch about our individual products or services. This is strictly verboten at ANY professional seminar and it is not even a good idea to blatantly pitch your services at a seminar you create and sponsor yourself for prospects in you local community. Here's why.

Firstly, if you want to get a good audience, you have to promise something valuable...how to do something a new way...how to avoid serious mistakes...anything that is well worth the time of your audience to put aside their pressing daily business duties. If you don't deliver on this promise, you will have lost their good will and nothing will get it back.

Secondly, in today's consultative, value-added world, your message is no longer product and price, but the vendor's character. What better way can you think of to get your message of quality and character across than by giving away some of your good advice?

If I owned a frozen yogurt business, I would give everyone a taste of chocolate swirl. If I owned a deli, I would pass out samples of fresh corned beef, or Swiss cheese. We are in the intellectual deli business, so I try to give away treats of insight that are every bit as tasty.

And that, in a nutshell, is why we all do it. Some people give away calendars at Christmas time. Some give away key rings with their names on them. We, however, give away some of the fruits of our brainpower instead of advertising specialties.

Do I think that all advertising specialties are a big waste? Not always. But, in our business, there are few marketing tools that can compare with the gift of our own knowledge. That is one of the reasons that I never pass up an opportunity to give a seminar. The other is, it's lots of fun.

I encourage you to get in on the fun and build your business from it. You don't have to start big at a national convention. You can start small, in your own community. All you need are these four key ingredients:

1. A subject that you are really good at and that is interesting,
2. A potential audience in need of your words of wisdom,
3. A venue that is respectable and is easy to get to, and
4. Visuals and handout materials.

An interesting subject that is useful and that you know really well is the most important ingredient. I once spent an entertaining evening in the cockpit of a 100-foot schooner docked at New York City's South Street Seaport. An Irish balladeer, who had performed at an outdoor concert two hours earlier and less than 100 feet away, was passing his guitar around the deck for the less experienced among us to share our songs.

When one aspirant to the higher calling stopped mid verse because he had forgotten the words, our leader with the slight brogue chided,

"IT'S NICE TO BE IN THE LIMELIGHT, LAD, BUT YA CAN'T GET PAID IF YA DON'T DELIVER THE GOODS."

This applies to anyone who is thinking of giving a seminar. When you are starting out, don't wing it. Rehearse in front of your mirror. Then rehearse in front of your friends. When you are good enough to be comfortable in front of your friends, you're good enough to be a big hit in front of strangers.

So far as attracting a good audience, the Chamber of Commerce or any local business group is a good place to start. These organizations are always on the lookout for good topics. Ask them how you can meet their program needs.

You can set up your own seminar and advertise in local media, but this is particularly hard in the beginning, since you will have enough on your hands just preparing your presentation. Once you have given a few talks and subject preparation isn't as time consuming, then, of course, you can try to build your own following.

Location is not only king in the real estate business, but in show business as well. While you don't have to spend big bucks for a hall, the meeting place must have warmth, good lighting and acoustics, and easy parking.

Finally, don't forget the handout materials. PC EXPO notes that its biggest complaint from seminar attendees is that they have to take their own notes, poor babies. We are well into the era of post baby boomers who are very tuned in and turned on to high tech talk, but lack the rudimentary knowledge and dexterity of elementary pencil manipulation.

Also, these folks need constant audio-visual stimulation, so how about practicing what you preach and load that new copy of Microsoft PowerPoint, or whatever, for a visual workout.

That's all there is to it. Seminars are great fun and they are a great way to build your image and your business.

When it Pays to Just Say "NO!"

Time is money. Fire time-wasting customers and move on to more lucrative opportunities. Not every customer who pays you, increases your income. Here's how to pick and choose your way to higher profits.

*I*n past lessons we have discussed ways to identify and target specific prospects and groups of prospects. The flip side of that marketing process, however, is to recognize when all parties concerned would be better served by a courageous decision NOT to take on an account, or even to fire one.

That's right. Turn them down. Tell 'em no! Give back the retainer (Oh, no. Not the retainer...). Yup.

When the chemistry isn't working, sometimes it's just better to recognize a smaller problem before it becomes a bigger one, face up to an incompatible prospect and, as former First Lady Nancy Reagan used to say, "just say NO!"

Here are a few examples of how to say no to a client and what happens to your business and your life when you do.

In my own case, quite a few years ago, after completing several very successful articles, I had decided that my writing for a particular business publication had ceased to be worthwhile both for me and for them. My dear old editor had changed jobs and the newly-installed one thought that my style was too conversational.

My subsequent two articles were about as interesting as Al Gore's campaign speeches. That turned out to be the good news, because, in my humble (humble? moi?) opinion, editorial changes to the copy resulted in such inaccuracies that I was actually thankful that the stuff was made too boring to read. Factually, the material was wrong. Yet nobody called. There were no letters to me or "to the editor". Talk about effective waste management.

So I bit the bullet, cancelled my "subscription" and began a search for the publication that would laugh at my jokes, pay for my dinner and still respect me in the morning. I found another publication that was more fun to be around. Since then, I have written a cover story and well over 120 sales and marketing columns that resulted in hundreds of calls, letters and other accolades... terrific feedback.

At a seminar at a major software company's headquarters, a few months later, two readers recognized me from my column's photo. Every month several readers began to call, or write, and a few have since become friends. This is my idea of a good time, but it all never would have come about if I had persevered under the status quo and not had the courage to change accounts.

Ronna Cohen, another example, is an investment advisor who needed to say no to a client. She must be terrific, because her client base, the amount of new money that people bring her to invest, increases, on average, by over a million dollars each month. I don't know about you, but not too many clients have asked ME to invest a million of their bucks lately.

Ronna, through thoughtful planning, picks great investments for all her accounts, large and small. She is both a lawyer and an MBA who maintains a very dispassionate and professional demeanor (a lot like we VARs do, except when we have to make a 6:00 PM service call with a bootable floppy disk, or a spare toner cartridge).

She works for her clients the way we VARs solve our client problems, which is based on a series of goal setting interviews. Then, except to tell her about a recent birth, death, or bar mitzvah, there isn't much need for clients to speak with her very often.

At one point, she asked my opinion about a client of hers who was calling her every other day, questioning every decision she was making and constantly changing his goals. If he were my client he would be driving me nuts.

"WHAT SHOULD I DO WITH THIS GUY?" SHE ASKED.

"FIRE HIM!" I ANSWERED. ACTUALLY MY SENTENCE WAS A LITTLE MORE COLORFUL AND ALLUDED TO POSSIBLY

ERRONEOUS INFERENCES AS TO THE FELLOW'S ANCES-
TRY. "WRITE HIM A PLEASANT, BUT UNMISTAKABLE
LETTER THAT HIS NEEDS WILL BE BETTER SERVED BY A
WIMP AND KISS HIM OFF."

Ronna handled it with a little more style than I would
have. She called the client to her office for an exit conference and explained that her time was her resource inventory
and, like any inventory, it had to be priced in line with the
value of the finished product.

Her client was given choices. He could re-subscribe
to the program she had prepared for him, or he could pay a
lot more for extra helpings of her time inventory that would
not improve his results. Or he could go elsewhere and, for
the same money, buy lots of time from someone who didn't
value himself very highly. In 1972, when I first decided to
leave AT&T, I asked my attorney why he had decided on
private practice rather than hook up with a large law firm. I
had never considered myself an entrepreneur and urgently
needed an entrepreneur's perspective.

"Did you do it for the money?" I asked.

"No, not for the money." he replied. "I could make
more money in a large firm, but in a large firm you have to
take a lot of guff (not the real term) from senior partners
and clients. In my own firm, I wanted the freedom to tell
you, or any client to go fan himself (not the real phrase) if I
wanted to, without being fired."

Good point, I thought, and opened my first office.

Through the years, I have had periods of greater and
lesser prosperity, and I know, more than anybody, that when
the going gets tough, the tough tend to get cheaper, but that
trend usually leads to the poorhouse. What is really needed
for those of us who sell ideas is the same as those who sell

hard goods. We need to take stock of our inventory once in a while and do some serious re-pricing.

Part of the marketing mission is to determine what the market wants and needs, and find cost-effective and profitable means to bring out our products to meet those wants and needs.

There's an old joke about Sammy and his partner Harry who sell yard goods to the garment industry. One day Sammy runs into the office and says,

> "HARRY, HARRY, I JUST SOLD A MILLION YARDS OF #756 CLOTH."
>
> "GREAT," SAYS HARRY, "HOW MUCH DID YOU GET FOR IT?"
>
> "SIXTY-TWO CENTS A YARD," SAYS SAMMY.
>
> "SIXTY-TWO CENTS!? WHAT ARE YOU, NUTS!? THAT CLOTH COSTS US SIXTY-FOUR CENTS!"
>
> "DON'T WORRY," SAYS SAMMY, "WE'LL MAKE IT UP IN VOLUME.

Our time and our thoughts are inventory, just like that cloth, and we can't sell ourselves short. Part of our marketing strategy must be the thoughtful consideration of how much creativity we are capable of, how much that creativity is worth to the marketplace, and how much we are willing to accept for it, both in suffering as well as money.

About two weeks after Ronna's interview with the troublesome client, a letter came in the mail. In it, he had carefully written down his goals and a request that she would take him back without a lot of discussion and just do what she does best, invest. Enclosed was a check for $500,000. Way to go!

Fools Don't Only Show Up in April

Broadcast fax? Email SPAM? Avoid the downside, and learn a better way. There are lots of effective ways to reach markets and a few really dumb ones. Here's how to tell the difference.

A few years ago, in a published article, a securities analyst named David R. Korus unfairly accused Dell Computer Corporation of inflating its reported profits by not taking into account foreign exchange activity on a quarterly basis instead of annually.

It seemed to me that Mr. Korus was putting the kidder back in Kidder, Peabody (which ultimately kidded itself into oblivion), because, if the results in the *New York Times* are accurate, Korus really didn't have a clue as to what he was talking about. So, when the Securities and Exchange Commission completed its expensive investigation of Dell's accounting practices, guess what? Use of the accounting methods championed by Korus (the kidder), instead of the way Dell does it, resulted in Dell being worth an additional million bucks.

So the SEC put some of our time and money, yours and mine, into delaying Dell's sale of four million new shares of stock while it investigated, and then Dell's over-the-counter price for said new stock rose 30%, or about 50 million big ones. Since then, Dell has sold so many of its computers that its stock has grown eight fold.

From a marketing standpoint, this Korus Kaper was only marginally bad for Kidder, Peabody, but it was great for Dell. The Kidder folks may have strengthened our resolve not to listen to Wall Street pundits, but the image of Michael Dell grows as the great business manager we all love to love. Way to go, Michael!

The good people at Dell may not suffer fools gladly, but they always seem to take pains to present the right, comforting image to us in spite of bad press. The Dell method would prove instructive to others who aren't as careful at image self-preservation. Immediately after the Kidder incident, Dell went before the press and explained his short-term and long-term vision and how he planned to reach it. He did reach it and still does.

His shareholders - those of them who bought Dell for the long haul - all did very, very well. The fair-weather friends who take tips from overnight pundits, and who buy and sell stock with the fickleness of the winds, however, took a pounding. Not just for this, but for many reasons, Kidder kids no more.

Perhaps the lesson here is that if we try to build our own brand image at the expense of others, we had better be right, or else... And it helps not to try to win converts by being rude and obnoxious.

For instance, take a company that introduced itself to me in the most uninspiring way. Well, maybe you should read my actual letter back to them, which explains all. In fact, I don't make a habit of wasting my time ranting at morons, but, in this case, I have made this letter a generic word processing document to be sent to everyone who now sends us that really dumb junk fax:

Dear Mr. X:

Perhaps you are unaware of the fact that is unlawful to send unsolicited FAX mail to recipients in the State of Connecticut, as well as in many other states. Violation of this law carries severe financial penalties.

In addition to your breaking the law, do you realize how annoying it is to receive unannounced price lists on my FAX machine every few days from someone I don't even know? I don't know about your buying habits, but it is my experience that I would rather buy from someone who is nice to me rather than someone who gets me annoyed as you have done.

While we're at it, can you imagine how stupid it looks to me to receive a FAX from you announcing "special prices for you only!!!" and hand addressed simply to "Purchasing Manager" whose name you don't even know. I don't know who your salesman Mr. N. is, but, from the way you do business, I don't trust him already.

In fact, I called Mr. N., and asked him how he got our FAX number. He actually had the gall to tell me that, according to your computer, we are already a customer of yours (although he could not tell me what we purchased, when, for how much, or if we ever paid you). Imagine that! I don't have any record of a purchase order to you, a bill from you, or a check to you, yet Mr. N. thinks he can convince me that we have a business relationship I can count on.

It would seem to me, that, if you really want me to buy something from you, then you would at least have the courtesy of introducing yourself to me before clogging up my FAX machine with stuff the mail room people end up throwing away, anyway. After all, if the truth be known, I am not a really difficult person to talk to. My friends think I am really swell and even members of my family love me (at least, some of them say they do).

Before I consider what you have to sell, I just want to know with whom I am dealing. I'd like to know that you are decent, too, and that you are more than a nameless, faceless check cashing service in another state who will take my money and leave me high and dry. Is that too much to ask?

You know, Mr. X, we are always on the lookout for quality sources. If you meet the quality qualification, why not approach me in a professional manner? Try a letter, with a reference, or two, and something that gives me confidence that you are a real company instead of a bunch of bozos. Then call me and see if I am satisfied with who you are, whether I am willing to deal with you, and take a few moments to learn what products I might need from you.

In the meantime, please do not allow your salesman Mr. N., or anyone in your organization, to send me any more FAX messages without my expressed authorization.

Sincerely,

Stan Rosenzweig

President

Some of the telemarketing/telefaxing methods I've seen recently remind me of a story of two stock brokers, Harry and James, who phone canvass stock tips to farmers in the Midwest in the hopes of selling them the stock they are touting.

"I'VE GOT THIS GREAT STOCK," SAYS HARRY TO JAMES. "I THINK IT'S GOING TO TRIPLE IN VALUE BY THE END OF THE QUARTER."

"Sure," says James. "I have a better great stock that
will quadruple in value by the end of the
month."

"Oh yeah," says Harry. "Well, I'm so sure of my
stock that I sold 200 shares to my mother."

At this news, James jaw drops open in amazement.

"Harry," he admonishes, "not your mother. Have
you no shame?"

This story gets a good chuckle in security brokerage circles where they all know that you should never believe what you are telling others. I can't help but wonder, though, if there is something in there for the rest of us.

I was at a VAR sales seminar last year where somebody got up and said, "if you can't sell them, FAX them into submission." I thought, who are these guys? Goodfellas? Who are they selling to who will actually buy from them? We all get these FAX messages and don't you just hate them? So, here's the burning question. If you hate them as much as I do, why do you think you can send them to others and still make a living? Can't you think of a better way? Have you no shame?

It sure beats me, but I'll tell you this: whatever short-term gain you'll get in the sales department from "FAXing them into submission," you'll lose in the long term. So, if you want the sales department to turn in results on a consistent, ongoing basis, you had better start considering the long-term marketing effects of those loose cannons in sales and set yourself some firm image parameters before somebody gets hurt and shoots himself in the warehouse.

Beware the "Ides" of Marketing

Unfinished, untested ideas are as dangerous now as Brutus was back in Caesar's day. These common sense solutions to a few everyday marketing questions will show you what your prospects really want, and how to give it to them.

*C*omplete ideas…and other thoughts. When we read that Caesar had been warned to "beware the ides of March," back in high school, my first question was "What's an ide, an idea without the "a", three quarters of a word, an idea that isn't finished yet?" The teacher thought it neither funny, nor profound, but it got a laugh from the class, which was a win in my book.

By and by, however, as I got older and more serious,

contemplating the meaning of life and other assorted headache remedies, "profound" does seem more fitting and I have come to wonder how many truly great marketing ides are floating around the universe...ideas that just were never finished, tested, put into production nor profited from. If I may update this great quotation from days gone by, then I admonish all of you to beware the unfinished ides, or they will march right over you.

For instance, I know someone who has read my columns for over four years and has discussed many of the issues raised here. This includes one about testing new and expensive image stationery via FAX and photocopy, before committing to expensive printing (That discussion is in the lesson "Your Stationery Should Sell, Too" in *Marketing for the Masses*, 1999, by Stan Rosenzweig). This reader then went on to create a terrific (gorgeous, actually) logo that, unfortunately, comes over the FAX machine like a dense, ugly, black square. This is definitely an unfinished ide that doesn't get an "a" put on the end of it.

This logo is an ide that is so close to being a great idea that it hurts. What would it have taken to stick the mechanical on a copy machine? How much would it have cost to FAX it to somebody? What's the harm in asking your wife, husband, daughter, friend, etc, "How does this look to you?"

Here's another example that is worth remembering, although it came to us many years ago. One of my readers sent me a sample of his recent mass mailing based on my January 1992 sales and marketing column, that championed the use of the memo form instead of the traditional sales letter. For those of you who share my own sound-bite retention span of the MTV generation, or who may never have read those columns, I said a few lessons back that I have found that the memo format gets a greater response and return than a traditional sales letter, because it is not only different, but more personal.

Well, this reader followed my suggestion. He sent out a memo mass mailing. His memo was very well written, compelling and easy to understand...for those who could actually read the words. Unfortunately, to be honest, I had great trouble reading what a great memo that was, because, at first glance, I only saw what looked like light grey type on equally light grey paper. Since this was a marketing project that was inspired, somewhat, by my teachings, I took more of an interest than I would for ordinary direct mail and looked closer.

Inspecting the document closer with my trusty Sherlock Holmes magnifier, I deduced that the memo had come from a fine quality output, 24-pin dot-matrix printer, with a very tired ribbon that could very well have been purchased in 1982 and hadn't been in for its 100,000 mile tune-up.

The result was that the printer impacted the rugged nooks and crannies of the sculptured Strathmore paper with as much success as Paula Jones trying to leave an impression on Bill Clinton without using a lawyer. This was directly contrary to the point of my July '92 column that a mailing of any kind can be a great marketing tool ONLY if people can read it.

Now you may not see the benefit of rehashing this case, inasmuch as many of you have never even seen a ribbon-fed, dot-matrix printer. But, don't rush off too soon. Hardly a day goes by when you and I don't receive some sort of unreadable mail. It's getting worse in magazines and on the internet where "artists" are now embedding background graphics that make the message almost impossible to read. You can join this mad rush to colorful eye-catching wonder, but be warned that the medium may become the message, while the message gets lost.

Here's a third example of an idea that is only three-quarters finished. There's a fellow in the old West who keeps sending me demo disks that cleverly spew out over a dozen pages of tightly crammed text. The assumption of the author is that, if only I would invest as much time in his project as he thinks it is worth, I might come to find that his software might have something to do with what I do and might be worth my time. This is a case where, even if the product solved my problem (whatever that might be) the cure (learning curve) is worse than the illness.

Now I'm very glad that some six to ten of you write me every week asking for these comments and suggestions. Keep those cards and letters coming in, folks, and I'll do my best to help you get the most reaction for your action. However, these are not exceptions, but common examples that reinforce that, in spite of how really creative you all are, much like sending a new satellite into orbit, it only takes a slight change in direction to send your whole marketing effort off the mark and deep into outer space.

Here's an incomplete ide that I worked on myself. It isn't a complete idea, and I haven't thought it all through yet. You see, my town has almost twenty pages of listing for law firms in its Yellow Pages, so I decided to look at legal software as something we could sell along with our other things. One package looked very sellable, so I decided to test it out. I gave the propaganda to a lawyer friend who runs his own firm. After giving him a week to digest the material, I called him and told him that I would set him up with an entire system for free (lawyers love FREE) if he would like to be our beta site.

> "YOU WANT TO KNOW MY REAL FEELINGS ABOUT THIS?" HE ASKED. "I LOOK AT THIS AND SAY TO MYSELF, 'OH, NO, NOT ANOTHER NEW THING TO HAVE TO LEARN ABOUT MY COMPUTER.'"

Here is a case where simple, inexpensive, informal research shows that price, truly, is no object and the objection is entirely something else. Here's a friend who won't even take this stuff for free, because the explanation was too complicated and all he could see was a learning curve as big as Mount Everest!

For all those of us (including me) who, from time to time, take leave of our senses and embark on that great crusade to sell the unsellable, help the unhelpable, or bore our prospects with every tiresome detail before we even know if this guy's worth talking to, here's that greatest old idea (an ide with a real a on the end of it) that has ever been chiseled in stone:

KEEP IT SIMPLE STUPID (AKA the KISS formula)!

No matter how complex it is to build, no good program should appear too complicated to use. You can be as techie as you want to be, but not with the prospect's time. Here's how to sell plain folk like us who have too much to do already:

1. Determine what it is that is critical, necessary, or desirable about what you sell,
2. Tell what it is, not so you understand it, but so we all understand it,

3. Show how to get to the decision point without wasting more time, and
4. Remember, if we have to do any work at all to learn what you are about, we won't.

Here's another example of someone creating a bright ide that was just too complicated to be a good idea. That someone was me. I hope I learn from my mistakes and I hope that by sharing it, it will help you, too. Have you ever advertised in local business publications and felt like you were just pouring money down the drain with nothing to show for it? "It seemed like a good idea at the time," you say. I have lost thousands, too...exactly the same way.

I used to run a catch-all ad that listed the forty-seven different things we do to improve businesses, but I felt like the Maytag repair man: Nobody called. One day, the local ad rep came by and I told him that I wasn't going to give him any more business.

"YOUR BOOK DOESN'T PULL DIDDLEY," I SAID. "NOBODY READS IT."

"OH, PEOPLE READ IT," HE REPLIED. "YOU JUST DON'T KNOW HOW TO WRITE A GOOD AD. LET ME WRITE AN AD FOR YOU AND I GUARANTEE THAT YOU'LL HAVE SO MANY CALLS THAT YOU'LL NEED MORE PHONE LINES."

A few days later he returned with the following copy:

OFFICE TECHNOLOGY CONSULTING REDUCES COSTS AND INCREASES PRODUCTIVITY. IF YOU CALL 323-6070 AND READ THIS AD TO STAN ROSENZWEIG, HE'LL SEND YOU $20.00, NO QUESTIONS ASKED.

"WHAT ARE YOU NUTS?" I EXCLAIMED TO THE AD REP
WHEN I READ HIS COPY. "THIS COULD BANKRUPT ME!"

"NOT IF YOU ARE RIGHT AND NOBODY READS THE AD," HE
SAID. "OF COURSE, IF YOU THINK THAT PEOPLE DO
READ THESE ADS, BUT YOU NEED TO FIND A BETTER
WAY TO GET THEM TO RESPOND, THEN THAT'S AN-
OTHER STORY."

Boy, was he ever right. Another simple, but completely
thought-out idea. Now we keep our ads simple and I don't
feel as stupid about throwing good money out the window
on dumb ads that don't work.

Somehow, in recent years, we've lost sight of what
our parents, in simpler times, used to call "common sense".
We rush off to try out new ideas at the speed of light when,
in fact, it is sometimes more urgent to be critical than to be
timely.

So, take your time to review your marketing plans
carefully before you commit. Don't get complicated. Keep
it simple. Ask a few friends if your ideas are complete and
make sense. If you beware the incomplete ides of March,
then you won't have to worry that you'll end up an April
fool.

My Gift to You

The best way to find out what clients want is simply to ask them. Here's a script and a plan to call your prospects and find out what it is that they really want from you.

*T*elemarketing Research. The best way to determine what to sell to our clients and prospects, I believe, is simply to ask them. Here's one way we do it.

Firstly, periodically, we send out a broadcast fax to selected individuals in our database. Not everyone, mind you. Just those with whom we have a dialogue and who we think could be insightful and helpful in our quest for market knowledge.

The fax is usually a simple one-page questionnaire that offers a "valuable free mystery gift" for responses…in addition to our undying gratitude. One recent fax asked these questions about each of three new services:

1. Do you think we should offer this service?
2. Would you be interested in purchasing it from us?
3. Who do you recommend that we sell this to?
4. Can we use your name as a reference when calling #3?

We then described our "valuable free mystery gift" as "the handiest and most useful desk accessory I have ever used or owned" and requested that the questionnaire recipient confirm the address where the gift should be sent.

We had a 61% response to this targeted list with valuable mystery gift. Interestingly, response to this questionnaire took as little as a few hours to as long as two months, proving that:

1. Some people spend the night sleeping at the office in order to get faxes at 3:00 AM.
2. Some people don't read their faxes until the end of the next fiscal quarter.

No matter, the response was great and the information was greater. I learned that we would not increase our sales and profits dramatically among our clients by augmenting our services with one product, but that we another would be welcomed with open arms.

Customized letters that are broadcast faxed to existing clients and friends can be a real marketing winner, but broadcasting to total strangers is not. In most jurisdictions, it is downright unlawful and there are stiff penalties if people complain.

Instead of rude broadcast faxing to expand our reach into new markets, we have instituted a telemarketing research effort that asks similar questions of strangers that our faxes ask of our friends.

Our purpose is, not to sell, but, to determine what these companies need that we can provide efficiently, honorably and cost effectively. To ensure that this is a market research activity that produces accurate results, we do not hire seasoned salespeople to do telephoning.

Instead, we choose at-home parents who have children in school during the mornings, personable retired persons who want to keep busy a few hours a week, and students who want a few hours of after-school work.

Many years ago, when I was a telemarketing trainer for one of AT&T's divisions, we found that research results were best obtained by hiring part-timers working only a few hours a day. Full-timers tend to get tired after five or six hours of calling and this has an effect on the results. There is no selling, so any gregarious person with a few hours to spare can jump right in and be productive without significant training.

Notice a few key points in our lengthy, but easy to use script:

1. We start by identifying ourselves, who we work for and what we want. I have found that this immediate revelation calms the subject's suspicions and keeps him/her on the phone longer.
2. We ask for ten minutes and offer something of value in return for answering our questions. If the subject has the time to spare and is the right person, this creates a bond that keeps the subject on the phone for the entire survey (most of the time).
3. We verify if, in fact, this is the right person that we should be speaking with. How many times have you

or your salesmen interviewed the kindest, gentlest, most cooperative person who turned out to be the wrong person? Marketing 101 says always confirm that you are talking to the right person.

4. If the subject is wary, or belligerent, and starts to treat this as an unwanted sales call, we make one attempt to satisfy his/her concerns. If this doesn't work, we don't make a career out of changing his mind. We don't want to win this battle at the expense (in lost production time) of losing the war. If one attempt doesn't do it, time to move on.

5. We confirm the recipient's name, title and address, in order to validate our database and, also, to remind the subject of the valuable gift in exchange for his/her cooperation.

6. We intersperse our questions with facts and questions that will get the subject thinking about how we can be of help down the road when our salesman does call.

The results of this marketing survey are:

1. We learn more about our marketplace and what we should be selling.

2. We learn more about our prospects and how to sell to them.

3. We develop actual leads for sales follow up.

You can use this same market research format with the same great results. Just replace our target questions with your own and let me know how you make out.

An Office Technology Consulting, Inc. sample telemarketing research script:

"My name is _____ and I am with Office Technology Consulting, Inc., in Stamford, CT. We are conducting a market research survey regarding Computer Telephone Integration and would like your help.

"If you can spend the next ten minutes to answer a few research questions, we would like to send you a free and valuable desk set, or $10.00 worth of telephone travel calls for your personal use. Are you the person responsible for making computer networking and telephone system decisions?"

If answer is no, ask: "Who is the person who makes computer and telephone decisions? What is his/her extension number? When is he/she available? Can you transfer me?"

If answer is something like "Are you trying to sell me something?" or "What are you selling?", reply: "Our company sells a broad range of technology products and services, but that is not my job. I get paid to provide re-search to assist the marketing department in developing new products and services for the business community. If you can answer a few research questions, we would like to send you a free and valuable desk set, or $10.00 worth of telephone travel calls for your personal use."

If the answer is yes, reply: "Good. Would you prefer the desk set that consists of a letter opener, a ruler and a fancy paper clip dispenser, or would you prefer a $10.00 pre-paid calling card for your personal use?" Take down the party's gift choice, exact spelling, title and mailing address for the free gift. Then record the answers to the following questions:

"So I understand how best to ask these questions, please describe what it is that you do for the company. CTI is the integration of telephone services with legacy data systems to leverage existing resources, enhancing the value of the IS (Information Services) department to the entire enter-prise. Have you heard of CTI, or Computer Telephone Integration?"

"Do you know how it fits into the enterprise networking solution?"
"Are you trying to learn more about CTI in the enterprise?"
"Have you considered CTI seminars?"
"How much time would you provide to attend a CTI seminar (half-day, day, more)?"

"How much would you pay to attend a CTI seminar?"

"How could your company make use of the following CTI features?"

a. Ability to merge voicemail, email and internet data.

b. Screen pops with integrated messaging.

c. Ability to phone in to "hear" email messages.

d. Ability to use IP from the desktop to send fax, or voice.

e. Seamless integration of all communications between real office and virtual office (home, car, airport, airplane, etc.)

"Do you integrate any voice and data services currently?"

"Do you utilize any of the following, (specify):"

Frame relay

T-1 point-to-point

T-1 exchange access

Internet pipes (T-1, 56kb, frame)

WAN - Wide Area Network

other

"How do you optimize these services to provide the greatest return for your monthly recurring investment?"

"Would you be interested in cost effective solutions to optimize these resources even further?"

"What network operating systems are you running today (NT, Unix, etc.)?"

"What plans do you have for migrating and to what operating systems?"

"Does NT play a significant role in your company's future? Does Unix?"

"What telephone systems do you currently own? How old are they? When were they installed?"

"How many stations and how many outside lines on each? Are these adequate? Are you expanding or replacing any systems?"

"When is your next premises relocation? When is your lease up?"

"At that time, would you consider integrating your telephones into your data network, eliminating the need for a new phone system?"

"Who is your primary data network service provider? Are you satisfied with the service from this provider?"

"Are you satisfied with the pricing?"

"What would you like to improve in this relationship?"

"Do you have a term contract? When is it up for renewal?"

"Who is your primary telephone hardware service provider?"

"This questionnaire is almost finished and I want to thank you for being so cooperative. Now tell me, what technology problems are you now facing that you would like to see solutions for that are not easily available to you in the marketplace?"

"How do you plan to solve these problems?"

"Would you be interested in speaking with one of our CTI engineering consultants?"

"Would you like to speak with one of our Windows NT or Unix technicians?"

"Would you like to speak with one of our Internet specialists?"

"Would you like to talk to one of our internet marketing consultants?"

"Thank you for your time and assistance. Your gift will be mailed to you within two weeks."

That's it. It is a bit lengthy, I know, and not everybody will sit through the whole thing. But, if you sell the gift and the need for assistance, many do cooperate fully. This leads to better understanding as to what you should be selling, how you should be selling and with whom you should be spending your sales time.

Let's Make A Deal

· · · · ·

**At Last: The secret to selling success
revealed. As a salesman, I probably
wouldn't hire me. My technique is
lacking and my efforts are sporadic.
Yet, my sales record is terrific. Here
are my best, most successful secrets.**

I am not the greatest salesman in the world. Far
from it. I am not even what I would call a good salesman.

In fact, not to outdo Rodney Dangerfield, but, I'm so
bad, I can't even sell myself to me. Why, if I were to come
to me for a selling job today, most likely, I would turn me
away empty handed. It's true. I have neither the skills, nor
the persistence, nor the personality I look for in a salesman.

Yet, I (and lots of other terrible salespeople) continue
to make a good living against all odds. Most of us couldn't

make it working for large company sales forces with all their procedures and paperwork, but, as entrepreneurs, we end up at the higher end of the sales production ladder.

How do we do this? What is it that makes some of us so much better at increasing revenues than others, without the classic selling tools of the trade?

When Donald Trump wrote *The Art of The Deal* a few years ago, he wrote that much of his value was in his capacity to "read" the other guy and determine how much value each side brought to the table.

What secret skills are possessed by deal makers such as Donald Trump that differentiate them from ordinary salespeople? I think there are at least four and, now that the secret is out, I have been sharing them with seminar crowds for about a year or two. They are:

1. The ability to make and implement strategic marketing decisions in real-time mode,
2. The quick-wittedness to discern what is the true kernel or heart of the deal, while discarding everything else,
3. The quick-footedness to pounce on the opportunity before cooler heads prevail and the deal gets away, and
4. The willingness to take extra time out of your day (to schedule it), in order to think and rethink your strategic marketing analysis of your existing customers, prospects and suspects.

Deal makers know that opportunities present themselves when you least expect them and they maintain the constant awareness. Like hunters of prey, deal makers place themselves in the important deal arena so that they are more often in striking distance of those few deals that may have enormous consequences.

In truth, most salespeople never ever see big deals coming, or going. They are so involved with the day's stack of unanswered phone calls, or the perceived obligation to make new cold calls, that they never look around them.

Those new calls, of course, must be made. Deal makers who get rich do so by augmenting day-to-day, bread-and-butter business.

But they are aware that they must be able to switch gears at any time. They know, too, that one great deal is worth a thousand little phone calls. Has the phrase "keep it in perspective" been revisited recently?

Here at Office Technology Consulting, we still push our fair share of paper. We sell and accept smaller telephone and data network design projects...but we don't go out of our way to prospect for them. We only prospect for those bigger deals that will increase our business in a meaningful way. Reducing one client's phone bill by half a million a year...now that's meaningful.

This may sound trite, but it's the "deal maker" in each of us that promotes us beyond being a salesman. The very same mindset that makes me think I can't sell lets me know that, if there is something that each of us has that the other needs, we can make a deal.

Don't misunderstand me. I am not talking about old-fashioned horse trading, hondling, dickering over price, or even selling based on lowest price. I'm talking about learning how to pick and when to choose which deals are most likely to make your entire year. I'm talking about brokering the big size deals that you read about in the *Wall Street Journal*.

For people like Donald Trump, the key has a lot to

do with picking up the scent and knowing when to pounce. For me, strategic planning is equally important, not just once a year, but as often as you can budget the time.

We define Strategic Planning is the art of CREAT-ING, then IMPLEMENTING, new strategies that may enable you to attain EXTRAORDINARY GOALS. Some-times you pick winners and sometimes your best plans run out of the money, which is why you need to revise often.

It doesn't always work, but that is no reason not to do it. In recent memory, we have had three strategic plans that failed, but I had three that succeeded in ways that I couldn't have imagined. Had I not taken the planning route, I doubt that I would have half the business we will book this year. In fact, this is the best year we ever had, which is saying a lot, because that is what I report every year.

In my selling seminars, I have often surprised attend-ees by telling them how we reevaluate our client base several times a year for the specific purpose of weeding out (we call it "firing") clients who cost us more, in time and energy, than they produce. I got that advice from Stan Nitzberg several years ago before he retired as VP of Venture Capital for Citigroup.

Nitzberg reminded me that our time is our inven-tory and firing weak customers, prospects and suspects puts more of this inventory back into play for higher mar-gin sales...another reason why I think that this is another great year.

On the subject of selling seminars, you should at-tend more than one per year, even if it isn't one of mine.

That kind of renewal is critical for:

1. Providing new ideas and keeping you abreast of changes in sales,
2. Keeping you pumped up to sell, and
3. Bringing you back to basics and correcting simple judgment errors that reduce your overall closing rate.

I started this discussion by telling you that I really stink as a salesman, but I can still make a very good living selling. Part of that success is due to my early exposure to professional seminars which gave me just enough knowledge to be really, really dangerous.

That is why I now spend so much time, on stage and in print, trying to pass the word on to others. It is why, too, that I am always willing to pass on to you other programs that will make your job easier and more successful.

You need professional training. There are a lot of alternative offerings around. Learn why they say that knowledge is power.

If you want to do larger deals and take home larger paychecks, you will need to learn how to move in the big deal arena. That's why so many people belong to country clubs, isn't it? Why else would anyone want to play golf?

The passion of golf came up when my wife and I were first dating and trying to identify common interests, sort of. She said that she climbed mountains. I said that I skied. She said she rode bikes. I sailed offshore. Finally, in desperation, she told me she had played the game of golf...twice.

"Twice? Why!?" I asked, "Didn't you learn the first time?"

See! Right to the heart of the deal. I sold. She bought.

We merged. If I can do it, so can you. Please reread this course several times. Make it a part of your selling education and strategy. In the following pages, there is a form for you to send to me to let me know how you are doing. Fill it out and send it in.

Maybe there is a gift in it for you. Maybe it will make you famous in our next edition. Maybe, just writing out what you are doing will help you to become better at it.

I do look forward to hearing from you.

Reader's Notes—

Use the following pages to reinforce and personalize the lessons in this course to fit your business. Remember: *Selling is a profession that gives its greatest rewards to those who continue to expand their professional understanding with time set aside to invest in its study.*

Lesson One—Why Prospects Don't Buy
Five true, basic reasons.

_____

_____

_____

_____

_____

_____

_____

Lesson Two—Creating an Artful Sales Story
Referring to the method on page 10, develop a sales story applicable to your business:

_____

_____

_____

_____

_____

_____

_____

_____

Lesson Three—Soliciting Success: Part I
Never forget the top 10 reasons I won't buy from you.

_____

_____

_____

_____

_____

_____

Lesson Four—Soliciting Success: Part II
The flip side: What the buyer really wants.

_____

_____

_____

_____

_____

Lesson Five—Soliciting Success: Part III
How to find more people who will buy from you.

_____

_____

_____

_____

_____

_____

Lesson Six—When You're Too Darned Lazy to Sell
Five steps to a canvassing-free environment.

_____

_____

_____

_____

_____

_____

Lesson Seven—It's Who You Know
Build spheres of influence with professionals who serve your prospective clients.

_____

_____

_____

_____

_____

_____

_____

_____

_____

_____

Lesson Eight—Keeping the Message Simple
K.I.S.S.

_____

_____

_____

_____

_____

_____

_____

Lesson Nine—How to Lose a Sale
After winning the toughest sales, don't let the easy ones get away.

_____

_____

_____

_____

_____

_____

_____

Lesson Ten—Shut Up and Listen
The specific knowledge you need...

_____

_____

_____

_____

_____

_____

_____

Lesson Eleven—Mining Gold in Your Own Sandbox
Two tests and three ways to build new business.

_____

_____

_____

_____

_____

_____

Lesson Twelve—The Fine Art of Using References
How to get and use references to increase sales.

_____

_____

_____

_____

_____

_____

_____

_____

_____

_____

Lesson Thirteen—The Art of the Deal
The fine art of mutual satisfaction.

_____

_____

_____

_____

_____

_____

Lesson Fourteen—Direct Mail that Really Works
Short, simple and easy-to-apply secrets.

_____

_____

_____

_____

_____

_____

Lesson Fifteen—Doing Business with Clients Who Hate You
Three steps to getting dissatisfied customers to increase their orders.

_____

_____

_____

_____

_____

_____

_____

Lesson Sixteen—Making Educational Seminars Sell for You
Educate your customers and win them as prospects.

_____

_____

_____

_____

_____

_____

Lesson Seventeen—When It Pays to Just Say "No!"
How to pick and choose your way to higher profits.

_____

_____

_____

_____

_____

_____

_____

_____

_____

Lesson Eighteen—Fools Don't Only Show Up in April

Effective ways to reach markets.

_____

_____

_____

_____

_____

_____

Lesson Nineteen—Beware the "Ides" of Marketing

Common sense solutions to everyday marketing questions.

_____

_____

_____

_____

_____

_____

Lesson Twenty—My Gift to You

Find out what clients want. Ask them.

_____

_____

_____

_____